ROBERT A. M. STERN
ON CAMPUS

ROBERT A.

ON CA

ARCHITECTURE, IDENT.

M. STERN

MPUS

TY, AND COMMUNITY

Edited by Peter Morris Dixon
With Alexander Newman-Wise
and Jonathan Grzywacz

The Monacelli Press

Library of Congress
Cataloging-in-Publication Data

Stern, Robert A. M.
Robert A.M. Stern : on campus : architecture,
identity, and community / edited by Peter
Morris Dixon with Alexander Newman-Wise
and Jonathan Grzywacz.—1st ed.
p. cm.
Includes bibliographical references.
ISBN 978-1-58093-283-7 (hardcover)
1. Stern, Robert A. M. 2. College buildings—
United States. 3. School buildings—United
States. 4. Campus planning—United States.
I. Dixon, Peter Morris. II. Newman-Wise,
Alexander. III. Title. IV. Title: On campus. V.
Title: Architecture, identity, and community.
NA737.S64A4 2010
727'.30973—dc22

2010033745

Printed in China

www.monacellipress.com

10 9 8 7 6 5 4 3 2 1
First Edition

Designed by Pentagram Design

CONTENTS

PREFACE

PARTNERS

1969–
Robert A.M. Stern

1969–1977
John S. Hagmann

1988–
Robert S. Buford

1989–
Roger H. Seifter
Paul L. Whalen
Graham S. Wyatt

1999–
Alexander P. Lamis

2000–
Randy M. Correll
Grant F. Marani

2008–
Augusta Barone
Gary L. Brewer
Melissa DelVecchio
Sargent C. Gardiner
Preston J. Gumberich
Michael Jones
Daniel Lobitz
Meghan L. McDermott
Kevin M. Smith

CAMPUSES OFFER ARCHITECTS THAT RAREST OF opportunities: the design of a physical environment aligned with the intended psychological world of those inhabiting it. Academic institutions define their own educational missions, and buildings give them shape. But campus buildings also have an obligation to context; each has to take its place in the ensemble, each must reflect the historic roots of learning and creativity, while embodying the evolving ideals of its academic community.

This book, documenting our collegiate work, is also intended as a meditation on the physical histories of the various campuses that we have been invited to as architects. It is not, however, intended as anything like a definitive discussion of the topic. For those readers seeking a history of the American campus, I enthusiastically recommend Paul V. Turner's *Campus*.[1] Additionally, the Princeton Architectural Press Campus Guide series, providing detailed information on campus plans, buildings, and their architects, is an invaluable way for travelers and armchair travelers to understand the narratives of many important campuses.[2]

Architecture is perhaps the most collaborative of the visual arts. I wish to draw special attention to the contribution of my partners with whom I have worked closely on campus projects: Graham Wyatt, Paul Whalen, Grant Marani, and Alexander Lamis, along with Augusta Barone, Gary Brewer, Melissa DelVecchio, Sargent Gardiner, Preston Gumberich, and Kevin Smith. Their work and that of the many others in our office as well as collaborating architects and consultants is detailed in the project directory at the end of the book.

I would be remiss in not also drawing attention to the many college and university officials—ranging from trustees to presidents, deans and faculty, development officers and facilities personnel, not to forget students and especially generous donors—who have worked with us to develop the consensus that is essential to successful architecture and urbanism.

Like a campus, a book is a collaborative effort. I take great pride in the long, productive association with our publisher, Gianfranco Monacelli, and with his managing editor, Elizabeth White. Peter Morris Dixon, Alexander Newman-Wise, and Jonathan Grzywacz were also indispensable, working with me to organize the material and helping to keep me focused. Megan Glaves oversaw the production of new drawings for publication. Michael Bierut of Pentagram, one of today's most inventive graphic designers and a valuable collaborator of twenty or more years, has again designed a wonderful and lively book, working together with Yve Ludwig. Lastly among those whom I want to acknowledge, but who are by no means at the end in order of my esteem, are the photographers who have captured the spirit of our buildings, especially Peter Aaron of the Esto group; in an age of mediated communication, the photographer is essential to the discourse—indeed having the last word.

1. Paul Venable Turner, *Campus: An American Planning Tradition* (New York: The Architectural History Foundation, and Cambridge, Mass. and London: The MIT Press, 1984).
2. Jan Cigliano, series editor, *The Campus Guide Series* (New York: Princeton Architectural Press, various dates).

INTRODUCTION

The American campus is a world in itself,
a temporary paradise, a gracious stage of life.
—Le Corbusier, *When Cathedrals Were White*

CAMPUSES—IDEAL, INDEPENDENT villages that provide the setting for socially and culturally coherent communities dedicated to learning—are a distinctly American invention at once representing a search for a viable past and an embrace of the future. Given America's cultural diversity, the campus and the rituals it supports—from sitting on the Yale fence to walking the line at the Air Force Academy—provide an essential sense of community we crave but frequently otherwise lack, uniting people in a common pursuit of education not only as the path to personal advancement but also as a model for society.

Why all the talk about the campus? What is it that is special about a campus as an environment for learning? Why not just take classes in any old place, perhaps even online? Why all the fuss and bother? Well, those of us lucky enough to experience a coherently planned campus know that the college campus can be a very special place—a physical setting for a community sharing a common ideal of scholarship and sociability. In the helter-skelter of the modern world, with roadside strip malls, freeways, banal housing subdivisions, and the like, campuses present us with models of community that the commercial world seems unwilling or unable to support. For many Americans, time spent on a campus is the only significant time spent in an urbanistically and architecturally coherent place, in a community where the town plan and its buildings directly support shared social and intellectual values. For this reason, if for no other, the campus is a singularly important continuing project.

At its best, the college campus is the representation of beliefs, of the specific character of a place, of a community, of an institution. It is the setting for the continually evolving

LEFT
Irving Environmental Science Centre, Acadia University.

interaction of people and ideas over time. It follows, then, that campus architecture is at its best when it digs deep into culture in order to affirm, and sometimes even to reaffirm, shared values and ideals. While the campus plan provides the diagram of social and cultural intentions, its buildings and landscapes give them their visual identity.

To design a building as part of a collective whole is a privilege and a challenge. To be able to join with distinguished architects from the past in a conversation across time, one in which new buildings climb on the shoulders of previous accomplishments while reflecting today's optimism for the future, is an architect's responsibility second to none other.

The idea of the campus is uniquely American, but at the same time it is an exemplary illustration of the American way of inventively appropriating tradition—indeed, as often as not, seemingly contradictory traditions. If we look to Europe we will find great colleges and universities but no planned campuses. If, for example, we look at the Sorbonne, we can see that it is almost invisibly embedded in the architecture and urbanism of Paris. Oxford and Cambridge come closer to our campus ideal: they are made of distinct quadrangles, but they are cloistered and very private, almost totally without public space. Not only are there no direct precedents for campuses as we know them, but the very word itself is of American coinage. In Latin *campus* means "field," and it was not used in the collegiate sense until 1775 when it was employed to describe the bucolic grounds of the College of New Jersey—since 1896 known by the name of its host town, Princeton.

Not only are the word and phenomenon of "campus" distinctly American, but more significantly the very idea that a college should be founded with a physical plan deliberately bound up with its pedagogy is uniquely ours.

The first fully articulated realization of the idea and ideal of the holistically planned campus was Thomas Jefferson's. In founding the University of Virginia he pioneered a new type of university that was both state-supported and secular. Jefferson built his university between 1817 and 1827. Its plan and architecture have become a standard by which American campuses are measured, representing a new form of place-making: a nearly self-sufficient village dedicated to the common pursuit of knowledge. Jefferson's design for the University of Virginia followed a plan he first outlined in 1810, when he proposed that the trustees of the newly founded Tennessee College

erect a small and separate lodge for each professorship, with only a hall below for his class, and two chambers above for himself; joining these lodges by barracks for a portion of the students opening into a covered way to give dry communication between all the schools. The whole of these arranged around an open square of grass and trees would make it, what it should be in fact, an academical village, instead of a large and common den of noise, of filth, and of fetid air.[1]

By the time Jefferson was able to translate his conjectural campus into a reality at Charlottesville, he had given a great deal of thought not only to the arrangement of its parts but also to their character as works of architecture, which he regarded as an art of representation, an art of communication, reifying a curriculum and emblematizing an ideal. In battling the state legislature for funds to realize his "academical village" as he saw fit, Jefferson identified a phenomenon that ever since has characterized American colleges and universities—their mutual competitiveness and the role architecture can play in that competition. Pleading for funds for the as-yet-unbuilt Rotunda, the centerpiece of his campus concept, Jefferson addressed the penny-pinching Virginia legislature rhetorically:

Had we built a barn for a college, and log huts for accommodations, should we ever have had the assurance to propose to a European professor of [first] character to come to it? To stop where we are is to abandon our high hopes, and become suitors to Yale and Harvard for their secondary characters.[2]

The year was 1822.

Through the brilliance and rigor of its planning and the dignity of its classically inspired architecture, realized not in marble but in locally available building materials—red brick, white-painted wood, cast iron, and slate—the University of Virginia not only constitutes one of the great places in the nation, but also an ideal that has for nearly two centuries exerted a profound influence over American campus design. The University of Virginia's hierarchical grouping of academic and residential structures around a monumental grassy mall set a standard that still prevails, influencing many campuses that were to follow. Soon, however, Jefferson's concept was joined by a number of other prototypes from scattered, almost suburban, gardenesque arrangements, to hilltop citadels, to entire country villages. As a result there is no definitive model for the American campus, just as there is no national style for our architecture.

While the opportunity to conceive a new campus for a new institution that grows directly out of contemporary conditions—an opportunity so brilliantly seized by Thomas Jefferson—may not very often occur today, the task of adding to existing campuses is more important than ever before. Since World War II, the coherence of many established campuses has been challenged by a zeitgeist-obsessed approach to their development based on disciplinary methods of art history that has led to the view that new buildings are the environmental equivalent of art objects in a museum, each reflecting a prevailing stylistic trend deserving of representation. As a result, in place of a shared community of buildings, there is now all too often cacophony resulting from a competition between ideologies and isms. Occasionally significant architecture is realized, but in too many cases campuses are populated with a motley collection of mediocrities, suggesting that most architects, liberated from the culturally embedded languages of the past, have nothing much to say, and what they do manage to blurt out, architecturally and otherwise, is pretty nearly gibberish.

Ours has been a nation, a culture, that forged itself not by overthrowing the past but by reinventing it. From the first, ours has been a nation that makes its own environment over and over again as new requirements emerge, sometimes by innovating but more typically by amalgamating, cobbling together, and modifying. Our early architecture as Jefferson saw it adapted an ideal of the past to new requirements. He recognized that we build our political system, and our institutions, on the shoulders of the past. As we evolve, so does our culture. We greet the future with high optimism, but not without a sense of where we began, not without a sense of responsibility to the pact our self-created nation made with history. So, as F. Scott Fitzgerald put it in *The Great Gatsby,* his classic novel of American character, "we beat on, boats against the current, drawn back ceaselessly into the past."

Charles Edouard Jeanneret-Gris (Le Corbusier), *When the Cathedrals Were White,* trans. Francis E. Hyslop, Jr. (New York: Reynal and Hitchcock, 1947; New York: McGraw-Hill, 1964), 135.
1. Thomas Jefferson, May 6, 1810, (Jefferson Papers, Library of Congress) quoted in Mary N. Woods, "Thomas Jefferson and the University of Virginia: Planning the Academical Village," *Journal of the Society of Architectural Historians* 44 (October 1985): 269.
2. Thomas Jefferson, 1822, quoted in R. G. Wilson, ed., *Thomas Jefferson's Academical Village: The Creation of an Architectural Masterpiece,* (Charlottesville, Va.: Bayly Art Museum of the University of Virginia, distributed by University Press of Virginia, 1993), 43.

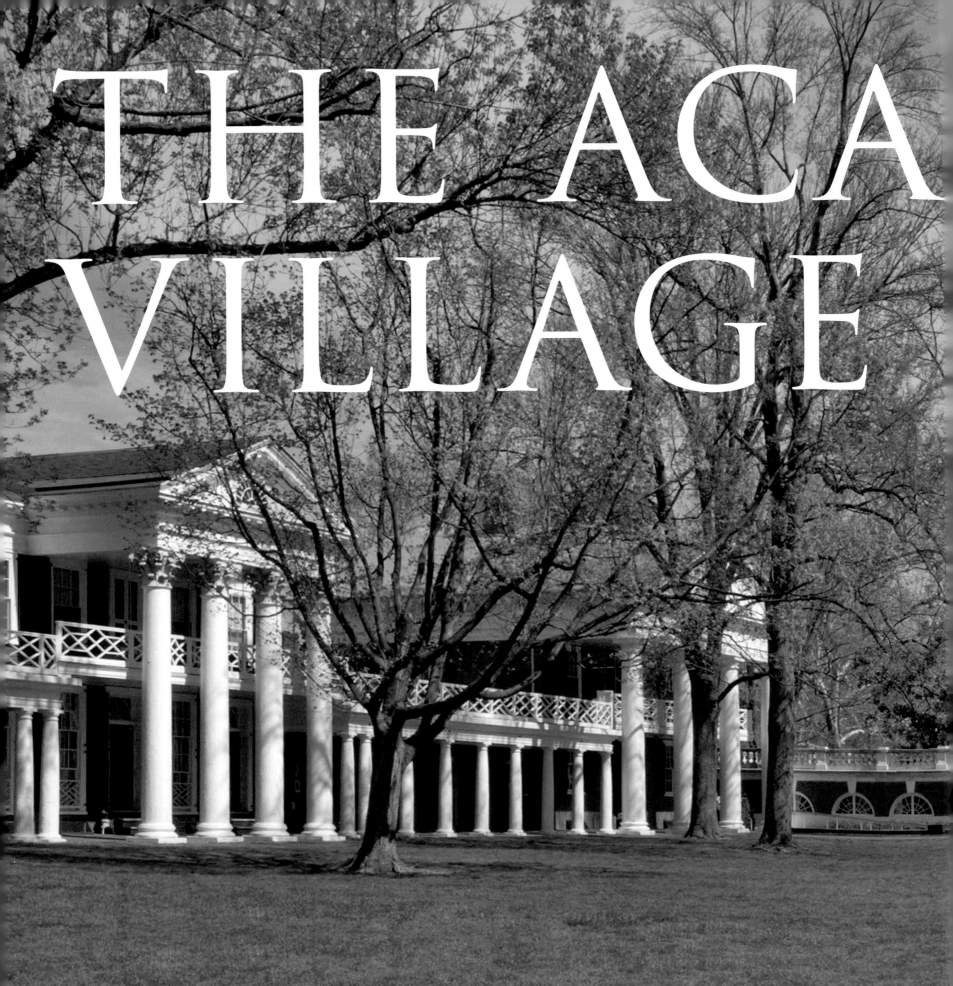

THE ACA
VILLAGE

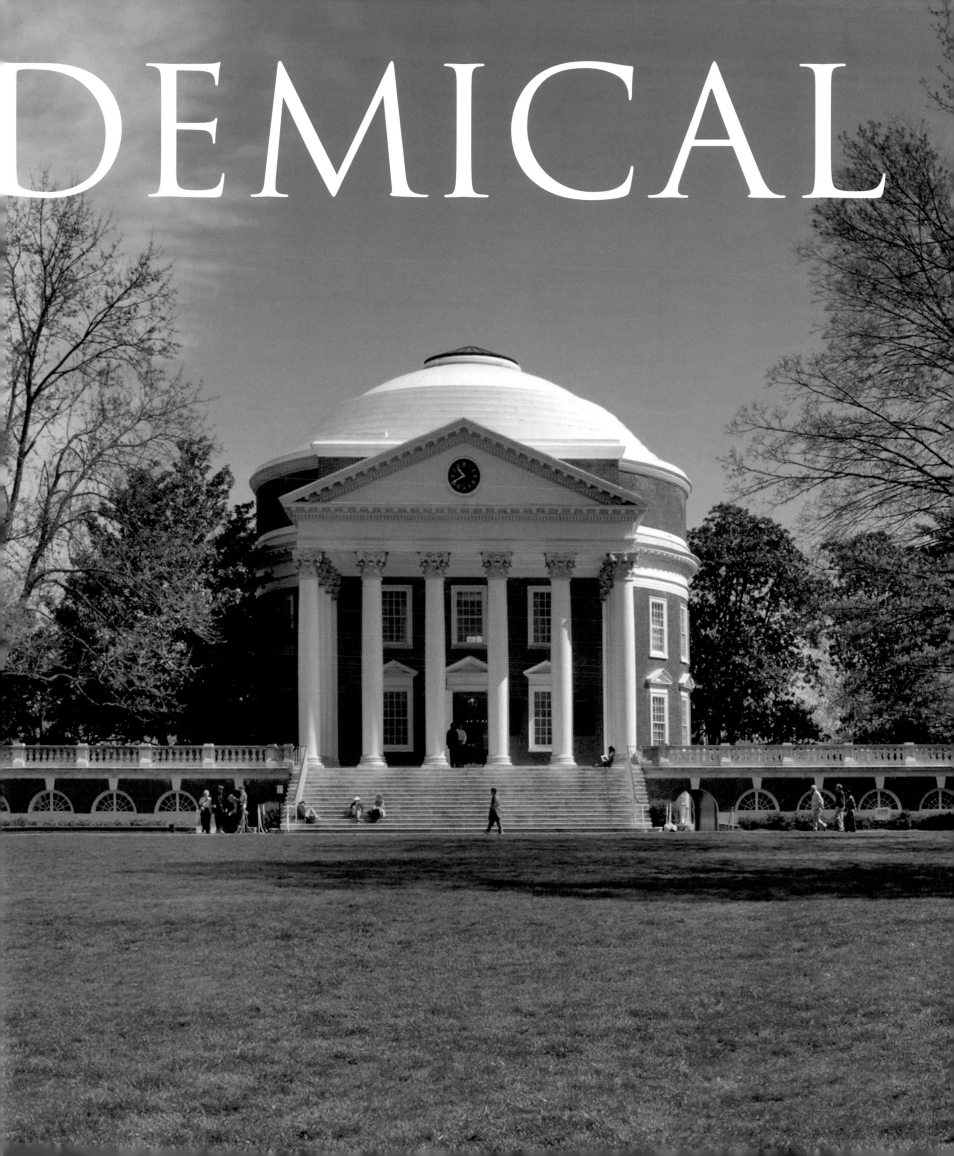

DEMICAL

UNIVERSITY OF VIRGINIA

CHARLOTTESVILLE, VIRGINIA. When Thomas Jefferson founded the University of Virginia in 1817, he not only inaugurated a new conception of higher education uniquely appropriate to our nascent democracy—a university rooted in a secular, as opposed to a religious, conception of society—he also shaped it as a learning environment unlike any before. Combining aspects of ancient and modern classical architecture and urbanism, Jefferson invented a new physical form, with its own hierarchical arrangement of buildings and grounds, finely calibrated to a clearly articulated curriculum and sense of public purpose. Jefferson located his "academical village" a mile outside the barely settled hamlet of Charlottesville, isolated from the bustle, temptations, and conflicts of a city such as Williamsburg, where he had studied and which he held in distain.

ABOVE
University of Virginia campus in 1856.

RIGHT
Aerial view.

BELOW
Jefferson's campus plan.

In conceiving his academical village, Jefferson did not innovate. Jefferson's brilliant design method was one of formal appropriation; nothing is uniquely American about University of Virginia's plan or its architecture. Nonetheless Jefferson was able to imbue them with fresh meaning to create a distinctly American place.

Jefferson's plan for buildings, gardens, and walkways is rigorously logical in its arrangement and picturesque in its effect. Every component in his composition had a role to play in a physical construct that marries architecture and landscape to the pedagogical and social mission of the university. Jefferson lined a broad grassy mall with pavilion-like buildings, all but one modeled after a building from antiquity, and placed at its head a library that was a half-size version of the Pantheon in Rome. Every other building—the ten pavilions lining the lawn, five on each side—was a lesson in architectural composition, elevating the idea of the campus into a carefully orchestrated public conversation about education, classical culture, and communal coexistence that extends backward and forward across time.

Jefferson's academical village was finished in 1827, the year after he died. The few buildings that were added to the university, especially the late-nineteenth century Gothic chapel (1890), ignored not only his architectural

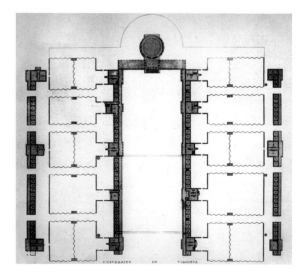

But in the 1950s, much as it had in the 1850s, the University of Virginia lost faith in its architectural self and lost its way. It did not embark on a bold program of high-wire innovation as Yale and MIT did, but instead contented itself with a sequence of fairly mindless examples of stylistic modernism and, as much to find room for new buildings as to escape Jefferson's long architectural shadow, relocated many departments to a remote site located a mile away, called the North Grounds. It was not until the early 1980s, with the arrival of Jaquelin Robertson as dean of the architecture school, and a change in direction on the part of the trustees, that the University of Virginia set out to return to its architectural roots. Sympathetic new buildings were inserted into the Jeffersonian core, and a bold redirection of the architecture of the North Grounds was implemented with a concerted effort to reunite new construction with the traditional architecture of the university as a whole. It was a privilege to be asked to participate in this important act of artistic and cultural renewal.

preferences but also his commitment to secular education. But when the Rotunda, which had been added on to in 1853, burned in 1895, bold action was required, leading to the hiring of Stanford White of the firm McKim, Mead & White to take on its restoration and also to design new buildings to meet the university's expanding programs. Significantly, in designing the new buildings, White did not impose a new style on the university but instead carried forward Jefferson's intentions into the twentieth century at a necessarily larger scale of construction. Further buildings in the first half of the twentieth century by Fiske Kimball and others sympathetically expanded the Central Grounds well beyond the boundaries of Jefferson's original campus. Still, the center held.

We were first invited to Charlottesville to consider the future of the Observatory Hill Dining Hall, completed in 1972 during the university's modernist dark ages, but by 1982 deemed an embarrassment. As expanded, our Observatory Hill (1983) was the first new building at the university in over twenty-five years to engage Jefferson's architecture in a positive dialogue. Porch-like additions camouflaged the existing facility and ameliorated the disjunction between that building and the university's Jeffersonian architectural tradition. The use of pyramidal roofs, arches, molded brick, classical columns, and painted wood trim combined with extensive steel-framed glazing established a scale and character that was at once modern and traditional—and most significantly, distinctly and deliberately connected to the vernacular of the place. Observatory Hill, sadly demolished in 2002, was quickly followed by a pair of small

ABOVE
The Lawn and Rotunda.

BELOW
Pavilion IX.

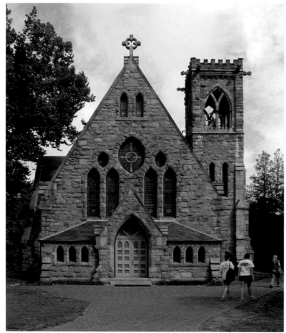

dormitories on Sprigg Lane (1984), realized as part of a design-build program that, though placing severe budget constraints on creativity, nonetheless resulted in stylistically sympathetic buildings situated in close proximity to a group of Jefferson-inspired dormitories built in the 1950s and Moses House, a historic nineteenth-century landmark.

After some years' absence we were invited back to Charlottesville in 1992 to participate in a limited competition for the design of a new home for the Colgate Darden School of Business (1996). Since the 1970s the Darden School had occupied a bland boxlike modernist building on the North Grounds, developed as a pair with a building for the law school. As a result of each school's growth, it was decided that Darden would build a new home on a nearby elevated site and turn its old building over to the law school. Our design was selected.

Set acropolis-like atop the natural crest of its twenty-acre site, the new home of the Darden School is anchored by Saunders Hall, a central commons building, and flanked by ranges of academic, faculty, and residential pavilions that mirror the village-like scale and character of Jefferson's academical village, with buildings realized in sand-struck Virginia red brick, cleanly detailed white-painted wood, and crowned with red-painted metal roofs. Like Jefferson's pavilions and Rotunda, the various buildings comprising the new Darden School campus are interlocked by arcades for convenience and a sense of community.

Recently we have been fortunate to once again work at the University of Virginia, with a new building, Bavaro Hall, for the Curry School of Education (2010). Bavaro Hall confronts the

Curry School's present home, Ruffner Hall, a bland modernist building of the 1970s, across a courtyard. While at Darden we were able to leave the recent past behind, with Bavaro Hall we were challenged to mediate between acontextual modernism and the Jeffersonian character of the nearby Central Grounds. In reply to those who protest that our approach "isn't modern," that it doesn't "break new ground," doesn't "advance" architecture, I reply that Jefferson created his design for the new University of Virginia by ignoring what he deemed the fashionable formalisms of his day, and digging deep into the roots of classicism. It is our conviction and also that of many in the university community that what is needed now, as it was in Jefferson's time, is an ideal that speaks with the authority of evolving culture rather than the momentary flash of individualistic experimentation.

ABOVE
Observatory Hill Dining Hall, renovation and expansion, Robert A. M. Stern Architects, 1983.

LEFT
Observatory Hill Dining Hall, Williams and Tazewell, 1972.

UNIVERSITY OF VIRGINIA
CAMPUS PLAN

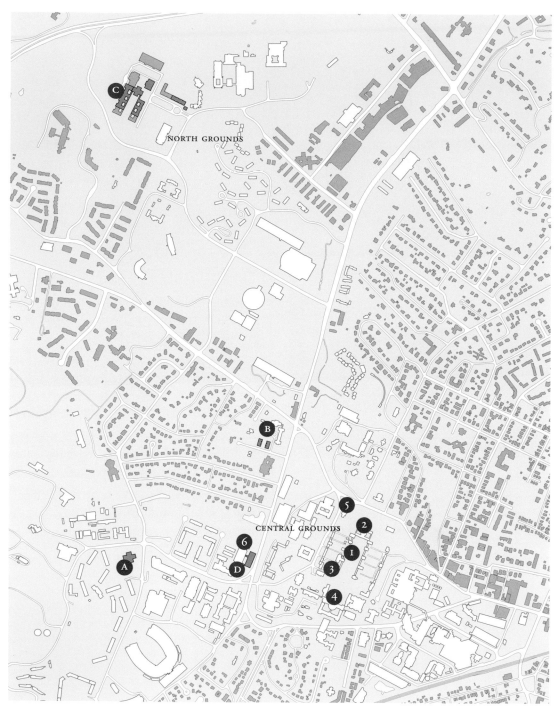

NORTH GROUNDS

CENTRAL GROUNDS

A. Observatory Hill Dining Hall
B. Sprigg Lane Dormitories
C. Darden School of Business
D. Bavaro Hall
1. The Academical Village
2. The Rotunda

3. Pavilion IX
4. Cabell Hall
5. University Chapel
6. Ruffner Hall

0   400   800 FT

DARDEN SCHOOL OF BUSINESS

1992–1996

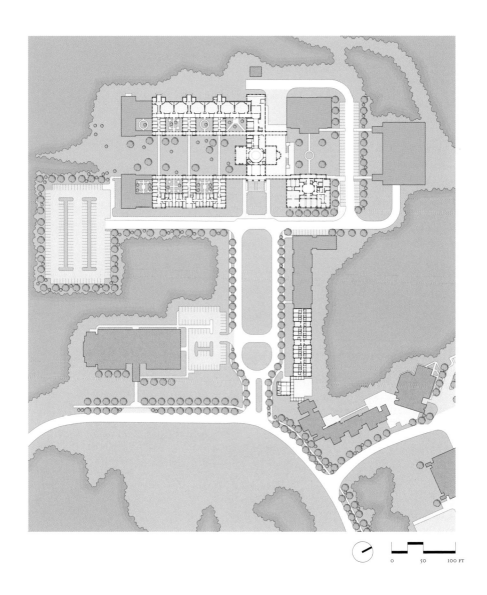

LEFT
Pepsico Forum.

RIGHT
Joshua Darden Boardroom.

OVERLEAF
South lounge.

BAVARO HALL

CURRY SCHOOL OF EDUCATION

2005–2010

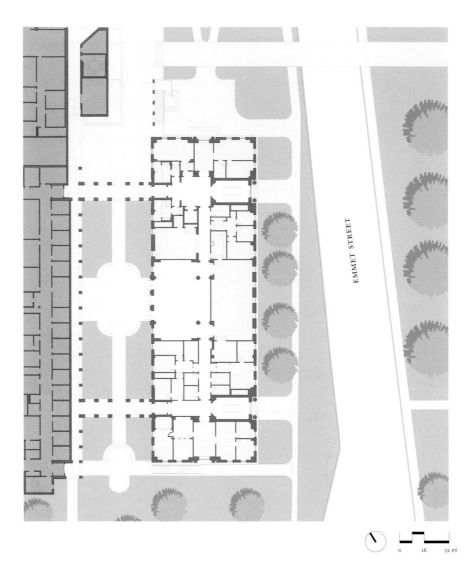

EMMET STREET

0   16   32 FT

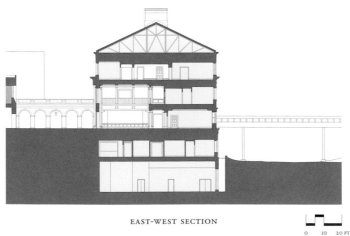

EAST-WEST SECTION

0   10   20 FT

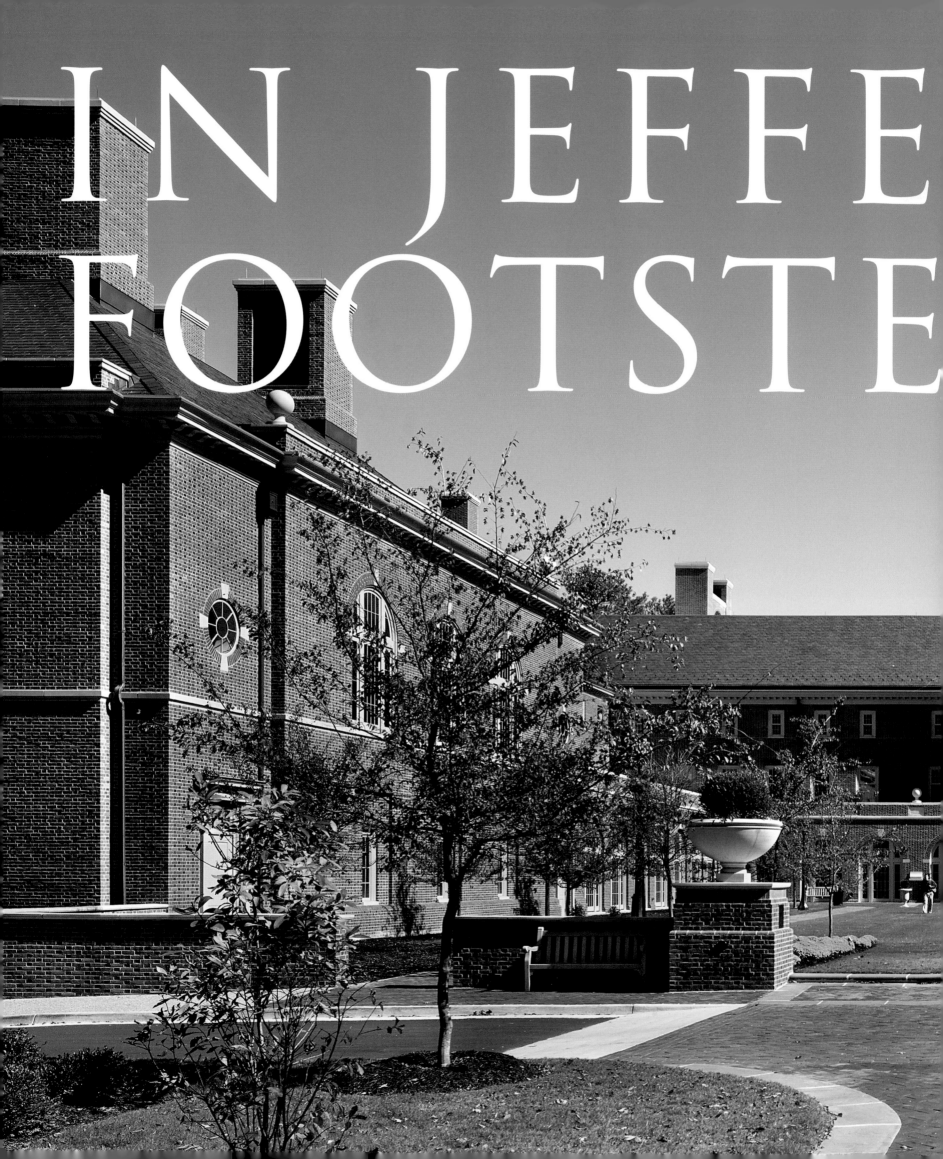

IN JEFFE
FOOTSTE

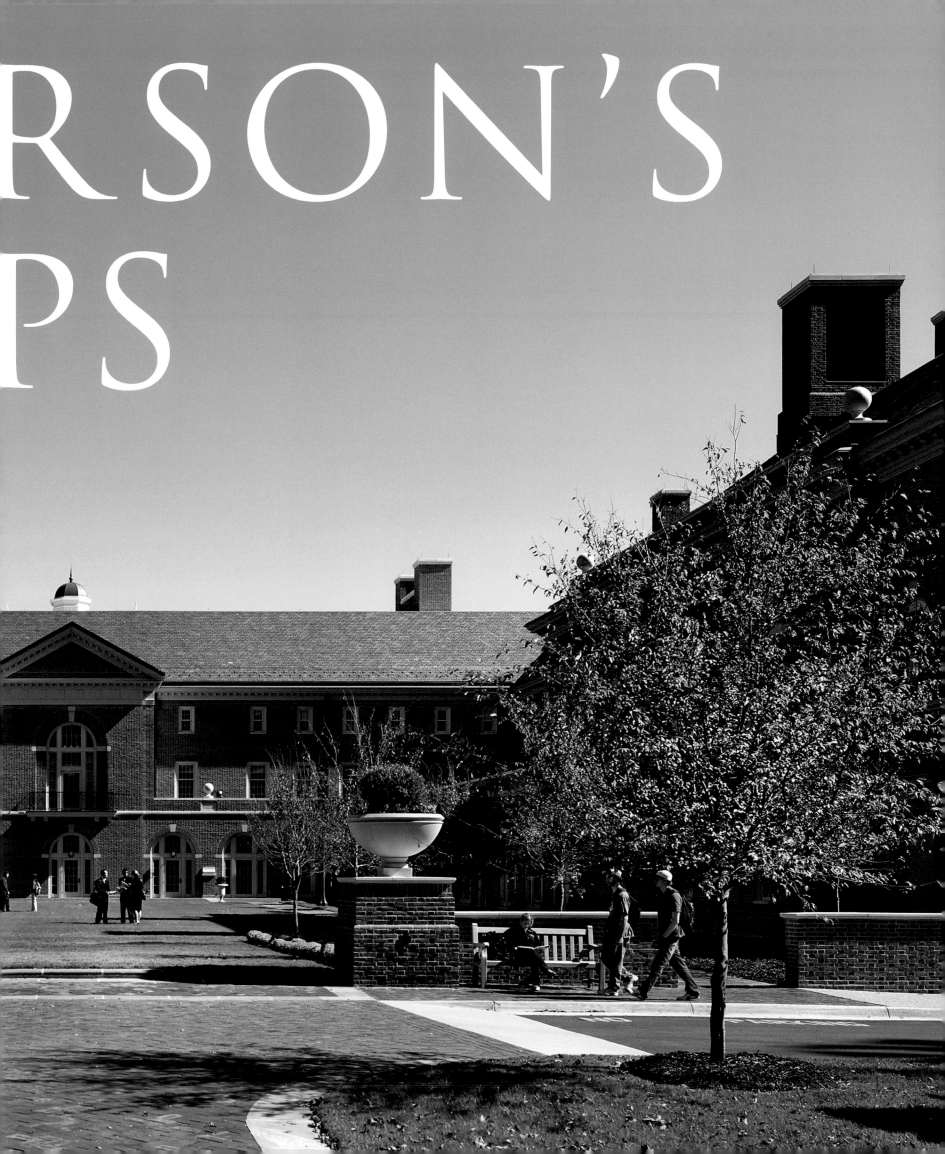

RSON'S

PS

THE INFLUENCE OF THOMAS JEFFERSON'S plan for the University of Virginia, designed as an academical village set apart from the distractions of urban life, extends beyond the campuses that adopted elements of his plan, whether its classically inspired buildings or its focal open space, to his belief that the setting of a university is not just a physical location, but a representation of the ideals of the scholarly disciplines that define a valuable higher education. For example, Jefferson, in very deliberately modeling the library at UVA after the Pantheon in Rome and making it the campus focal point, clearly stated that secular learning as opposed to religion was central to modern university life, thereby establishing a pattern that would be frequently emulated. And his choice of a rural area outside of then-tiny Charlottesville, reflecting a conviction that the university should distance itself from the distractions of urban life, was to play a significant role in determining the location for innumerable new colleges and universities.

Jefferson's plan for UVA was largely forgotten until 1895 when, after a fire damaged the Rotunda, Stanford White, then at the height of his fame and influence as an architect, was hired to restore the building. White was so impressed with Jefferson's plan that he used it as a model for his design for New York University's new campus in the Bronx, New York, and his partner, Charles Follen McKim, simultaneously at work on Columbia University's new campus in Manhattan, also adopted it. Jefferson's academical village continues to influence campus design to this day.

PAGES 40–41
*Fields Courtyard at
Miller Hall looking east.*

LEFT
*Fields Courtyard
from the Darden Gates
looking east.*

THE COLLEGE OF WILLIAM & MARY

WILLIAMSBURG, VIRGINIA. William and Mary, founded in 1693 was, as Paul Turner points out, probably the first college ever established in a "truly rural environment." But a nearby fortified outpost soon became the city of Williamsburg, capital of the Virginia Colony, and in 1705 William and Mary's original building was replaced by the so-called Wren building, shortly thereafter flanked with a new building to each side, forming an open quadrangle that terminated the axis of the capital's main street, thereby directly engaging the college with city life.

William and Mary remained a provincial college throughout the nineteenth century. Closed for the duration of the Civil War, it was shuttered again between 1882 and 1888 for lack of funds. The college didn't get going in earnest until 1906, when the Commonwealth of Virginia again stepped in and it became a public institution.

During Thomas Jefferson's student days at William and Mary in the early 1760s, Williamsburg was a sophisticated city full of the quotidian distractions that he would seek to avoid in conceiving the University of Virginia as its own village deliberately set a good distance from Charlottesville. Well before embarking on that plan, Jefferson, critical of William and Mary's worldliness, prepared an unrealized plan (1774) for his alma mater in which he proposed to close the courtyard facing the Wren building in order to isolate the college from the city. He also is said to have laid out the Sunken Garden behind the Wren building, a hedge-lined greensward that would direct the twentieth century expansion of the college inward rather than to its host city.

William and Mary's growth in the 1920s and 1930s followed the tradition of Wren and the red-brick Georgian of Virginia's Tidewater region. But in the 1960s and 1970s, the authority of Georgian precedent gave way to a wishy-washy blend of modernism and Georgian classicism. It was not until the 1990s that the college re-embraced its stylistic roots with the construction of Allan Greenberg's McGlothlin Street Hall (1995).

In 1999 we were asked to study nineteen sites being considered for the new home of the college's Mason School of Business, leading to the selection of one at the western edge of campus, where, ten years later, Alan B. Miller Hall was realized. Situated to bookend and mirror the Wren building, Miller Hall (2009), opens not to the town but to the landscape beyond, straddling an established path leading from the main campus past the Darden Gates to the Lake Matoaka amphitheater and College Woods.

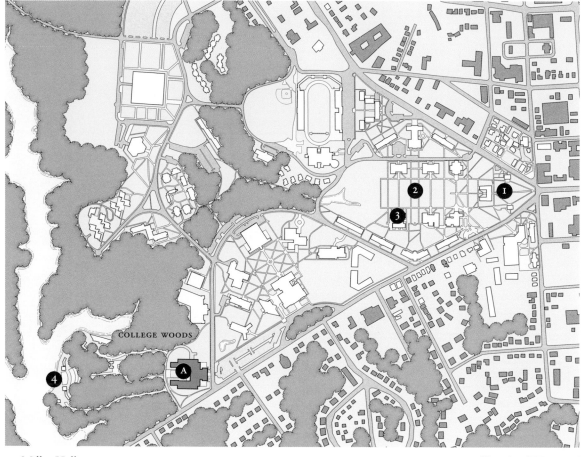

A. Miller Hall
1. Sir Christopher Wren Building
2. Sunken Garden
3. McGlothlin Street Hall
4. Lake Matoaka Amphitheater

0 150 300 600 FT

MILLER HALL

MASON SCHOOL OF BUSINESS

2005–2009

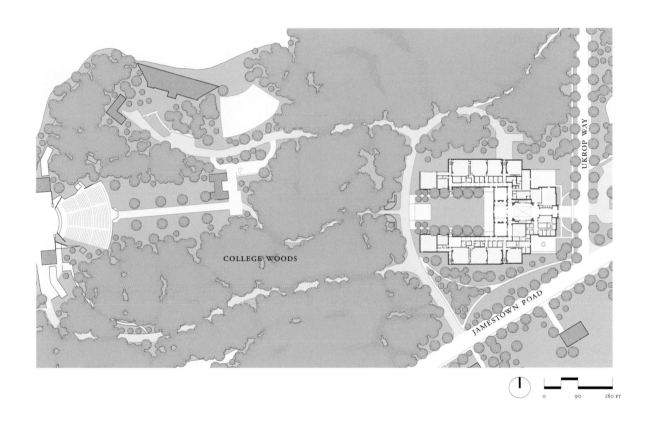

COLLEGE WOODS

UKROP WAY

JAMESTOWN ROAD

0   90   180 FT

LEFT
McLeod Business Library.

RIGHT TOP
Center lounge.
Brinkley Commons.

RIGHT BOTTOM
Executive dining room.
North gallery.

UNIVERSITY OF SOUTH CAROLINA

COLUMBIA, SOUTH CAROLINA. To achieve the ideal of a self-sufficient academical village required that virtually all the component parts be realized at once, something most institutions were unable to achieve. Barring that possibility, Jefferson's notion of modest sized buildings, each devoted to a different subject and arranged around a shared open space, could be realized over time, as was the case with the University of South Carolina. Founded in Columbia as South Carolina College in 1801, predating the establishment of the University of Virginia as a state-supported institution of higher learning, the college did not achieve university status until 1906.

In 1802 a competition for the "best original plan of a college" was held, and the submission chosen was that of Robert Mills, a native South Carolinian who was living in Washington where he was assisting Jefferson with his architectural projects. Mills supplied a design for a single building, as required by the competition rules. But by the time the trustees moved forward in earnest in 1805, a new plan calling for a central green surrounded by several pavilion-like buildings was adopted, anticipating Jefferson's unrealized plan for Tennessee College (1810) and the University of Virginia (begun in 1817), suggesting that Mills made important contributions to his master's work. Mills's South Carolina plan lacked the diagrammatic rigor of Jefferson's, but its clarity was such that, as Montgomery Schuyler put it, "architecturally simple, rational, and similar" buildings could be realized over time. Complementing the modest buildings along with Jacob Graves's Roman Corinthian College Hall (1853), built on a separate site south of the campus, Mills House (1825) enhanced the architectural prestige of the campus while

maintaining what Schuyler called its "character of congruity."[1]

For more than a hundred years, the university consistently enjoyed what Schuyler described in 1909 as "the rare distinction of a college yard . . . of which the total impression is homogenous and not confused."[2] But as the campus expanded after World War II, congruity gave way to stylistic competition, yielding a mismatched

collection of structures constituting an East Campus, where the first of our two buildings at USC, the Hollings National Advocacy Center (1998), is sited. The design of Hollings, a building dedicated to the training of high-level Federal legal personnel, rejects the dissonance of the university's recent past in favor of its historic "congruity." A simple building, Hollings suggests a village in the manner of Jefferson but with the principal building housing shared academic and social facilities and the linked pavilions accommodating bedrooms interspersed with study lounges. The entrance building embraces the classicism of Mills and Graves with a more vernacular approach taken with the pavilionated wings enclosing garden courtyards, embodying Schuyler's belief that on occasion

exceptional and architecturesque buildings may be developed to a much higher degree of ornateness without contradicting or putting to shame the humbler and more comprehensive erections, while themselves gaining by their conformity.[3]

A second building for USC, the West Quadrangle of the South Campus Housing (1997), squeezed between a parking garage and athletic fields on a site remote from the historic center of the campus, also embraces the monumental classicism of Mills and Graves. Consisting of a three- and four-story H-plan structure, West Quad was designed to attract independent-minded upper-year students who had been choosing to flee conventional dormitories for off-campus accommodations by providing four-bedroom apartments with the benefits of shared community facilities, ranging from offices for counselors to grandly proportioned lounges, and other social spaces.

1. Montgomery Schuyler, "Architecture of American Colleges VIII—The Southern Colleges," *Architectural Record* 30 (July 1911): 68.
2. Ibid.
3. Ibid.

ABOVE LEFT
The Horseshoe, 1805.

ABOVE RIGHT
College Hall, Jacob Graves, 1853.

BELOW
Close-Hipp Building (now Darla Moore School of Business), GMK Associates, 1973.

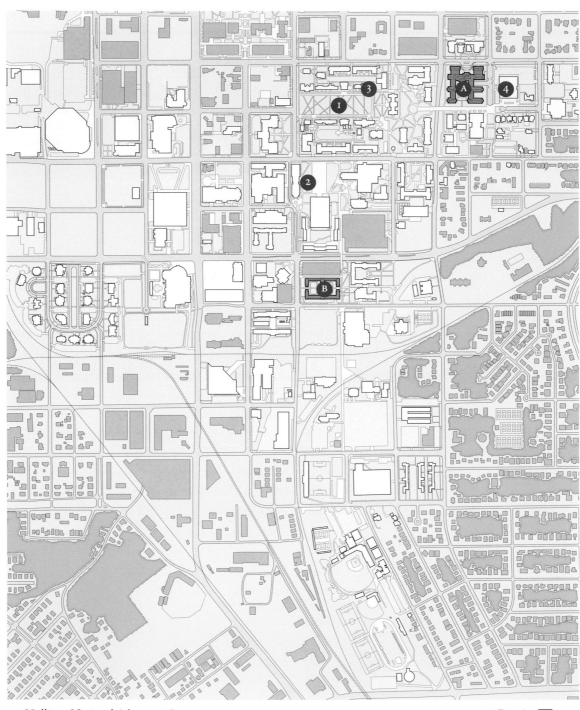

A. Hollings National Advocacy Center
B. South Campus Housing, West Quad
1. The Horseshoe
2. College Hall
3. DeSaussure College
4. Darla Moore School of Business

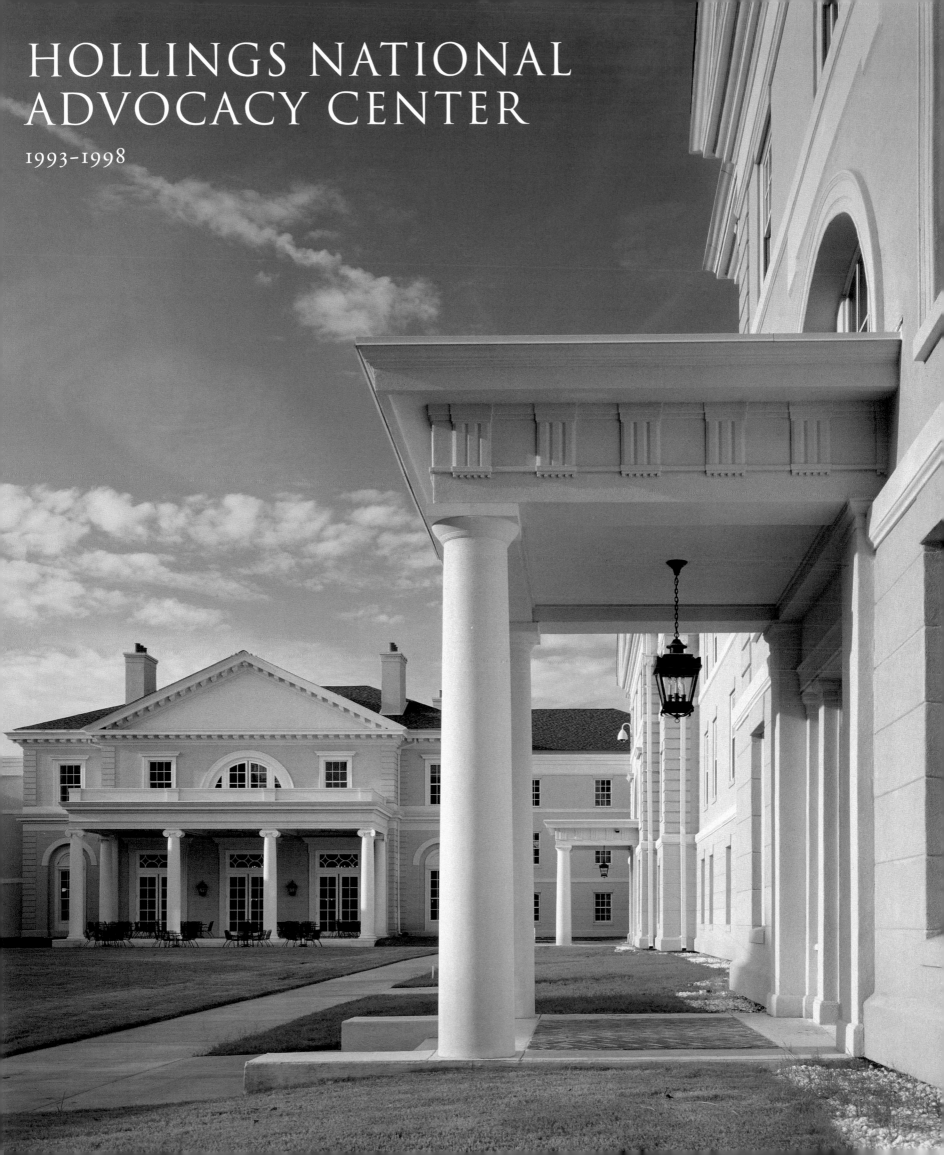

HOLLINGS NATIONAL
ADVOCACY CENTER

1993–1998

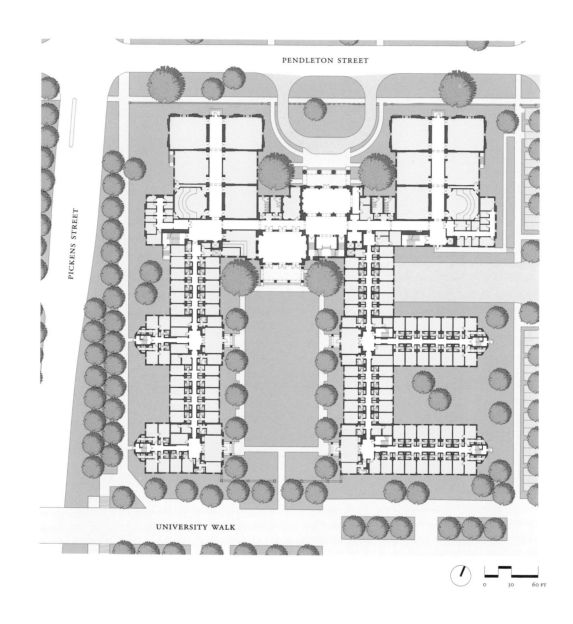

PENDLETON STREET

PICKENS STREET

UNIVERSITY WALK

0   30   60 FT

BELOW
*South courtyard from
University Walk.*

OVERLEAF
*Main entrance on Pendleton
Street.*

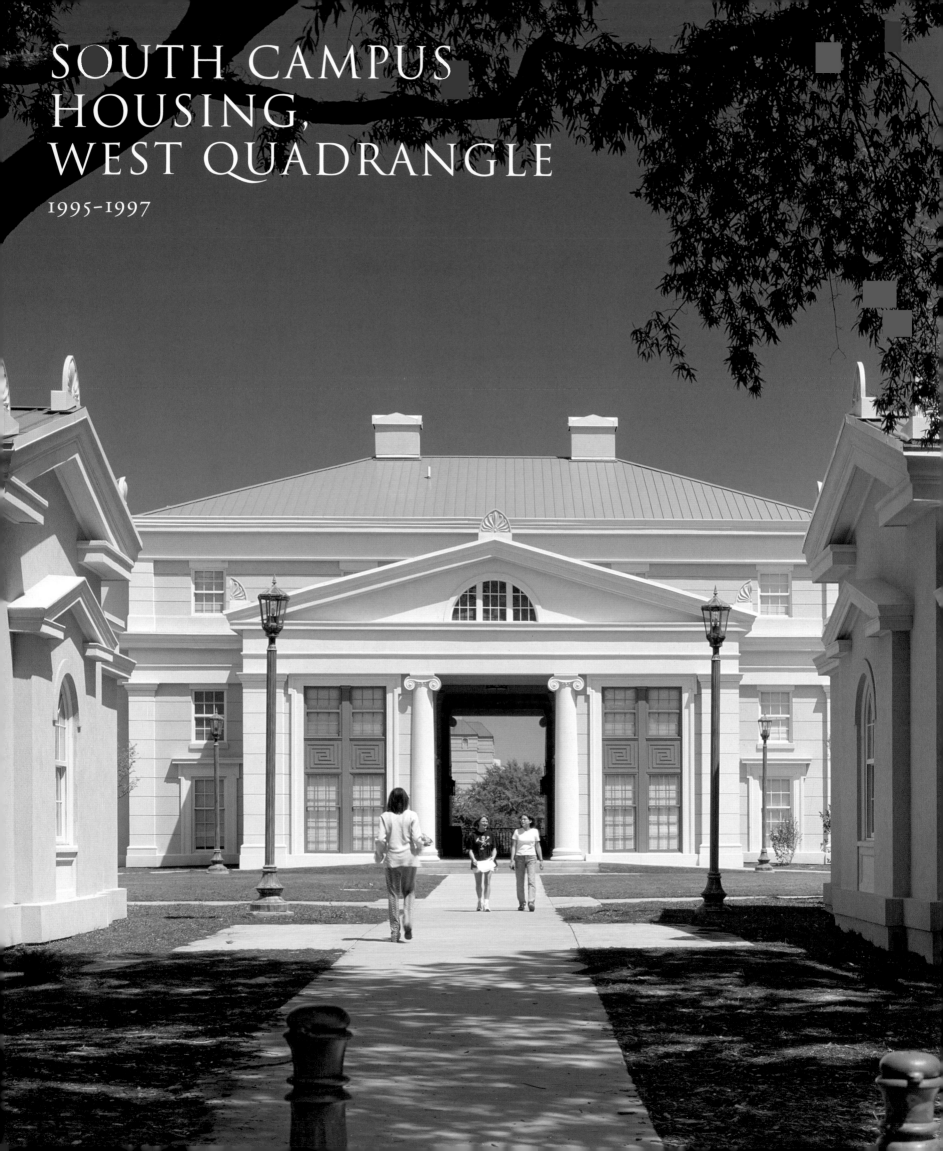

SOUTH CAMPUS HOUSING, WEST QUADRANGLE

1995-1997

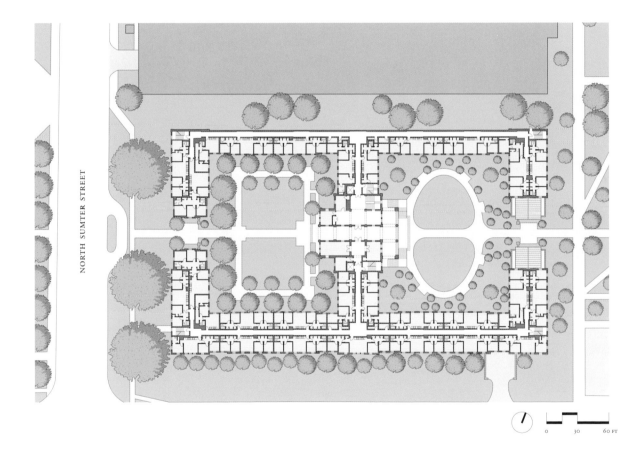

NORTH SUMTER STREET

0   30   60 FT

LEFT TOP
Lounge.

LEFT BOTTOM
Stair hall.

RIGHT
Meeting room.

WILLIAM GATES
COMPUTER SCIENCE

STANFORD UNIVERSITY

PALO ALTO, CALIFORNIA. Though at first glance, Stanford University seems conceptually and stylistically worlds away from the University of Virginia, it is, I would argue, the isolated academical village par excellence, a place apart on vast acreage but with the convenience of a nearby town, Palo Alto. In 1886 Leland Stanford, a railroad baron, former governor of and United States senator from California, founded a university to memorialize his only son and namesake, who had died two years earlier. To lay out the university, which was to be located on Stanford's eight-thousand-acre Palo Alto estate, he hired Frederick Law Olmsted, who drew up a plan incorporating domestically scaled buildings picturesquely distributed along paths winding through the hilly uplands.

character was established and a new university achieved its identity. Although an academical village, unlike UVA Stanford was cloistral, setting the stage for the developments that would take place at Pennsylvania, Princeton, Yale, and other established colleges as they burgeoned into universities. Only one of Coolidge's three quadrangles was realized, and under the iron will of Stanford's widow, Jane, the university grew in helter-skelter manner until the 1920s, when a new plan and buildings by John Bakewell and Arthur Brown, who were sympathetic to the original but not slavishly so, returned a measure of order to the

Disappointed with this inherently modest proposal, Stanford insisted on a monumental grouping on the flat plain below, and Olmsted obliged him with a residential and academic core approached along a mile-long, palm-tree-lined drive.

Stanford chose as his university's architect Olmsted's friend and frequent collaborator H. H. Richardson, who died before beginning work. Stanford then turned to Richardson's successor, Charles A. Coolidge, whose design for the main campus group drew upon his mentor's sources in the Romanesque architecture of Spain to describe a plan of three low quadrangular cloisters dominated by the steeply pitched crossing tower of the Memorial Church and a Memorial Arch that would have satisfied an emperor, on axis with the campus's monumental entrance. Both the church and arch were felled by the 1906 earthquake. The church was rebuilt without its tower in 1913, while the Memorial Arch was never reconstructed.

Virtually overnight, under Coolidge's leadership, a strong and enduring architectural

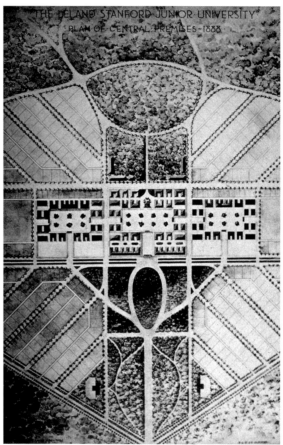

university. After World War II, however, connections with the past were cast aside under the modernist Eldridge T. Spencer, whose flat-roofed Stern Hall dormitory (1948) so offended alumni that the university initiated a policy mandating red-tile roofs on all new buildings and a material palette that respected, no matter how superficially, the warm sandstone tones of the buildings designed by Coolidge, Bakewell, and Brown.

In the 1980s, faced with the motley assembly of buildings and sheds that had grown up between the original quadrangle and the medical school, under the direction of campus architect David Neuman, Stanford set out to recapture its architectural heritage with buildings arranged to honor Olmsted's long-compromised campus plan. Some architects hired as part of this effort, like Arthur Erickson, resisted Neuman's efforts to regenerate the past. Located next to Erickson's Gilbert Biological Sciences Building (1990), our William Gates Computer Science Building (1996) embraces Stanford's historic pattern, demonstrating that a new building could be devoted to the most innovative programs in digital technology while participating in an architectural conversation across time that extends from medieval Spain to early-twentieth-century California.

Gates Hall is entered through a triple-height arch recalling Richardson and Coolidge's Romanesque. Around the corner, an open loggia provides the building's second entrance from which stairs lead down to a lower level, where three sloped-floor auditoriums and a variety of flat-floor classrooms provide the latest in interactive and distance-learning capabilities. Warm buff limestone and stucco walls, deeply

ABOVE
Near West Campus proposal, Robert A. M. Stern Architects, 1994.

BELOW
View from Memorial Quadrangle through Memorial Court.

recessed windows, and a low-pitched clay tile roof, reflecting the architecture of the historic campus, are overlaid on a steel frame that finds its visible expression in the window wall.

While the Gates Computer Science Building was under construction, we were invited to develop a master plan concept for Olmsted's unrealized western quadrangle that had over time been populated with some permanent and many temporary buildings. Our plan (1994), reconstituting Olmsted's and Coolidge's quadrangle plan to house a state-of-the-art high-tech hub, was not accepted.

STANFORD UNIVERSITY
CAMPUS PLAN

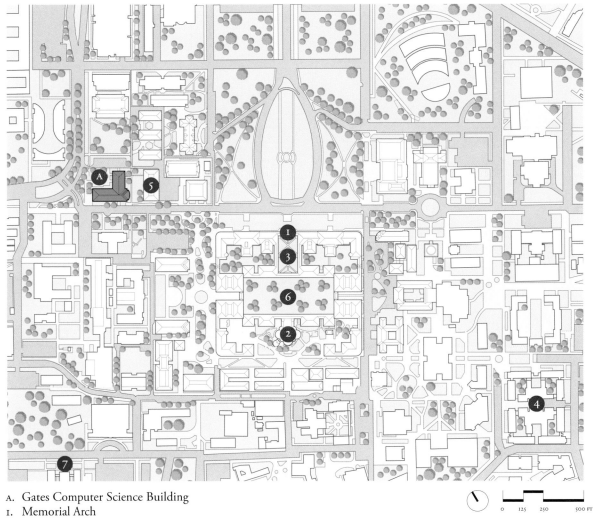

A. Gates Computer Science Building
1. Memorial Arch
2. Memorial Church
3. Memorial Court
4. Stern Hall
5. Gilbert Biological Sciences Building
6. Memorial Quad
7. Lagunita Court

0   125   250   500 FT

WILLIAM GATES
COMPUTER SCIENCE
BUILDING

1992–1996

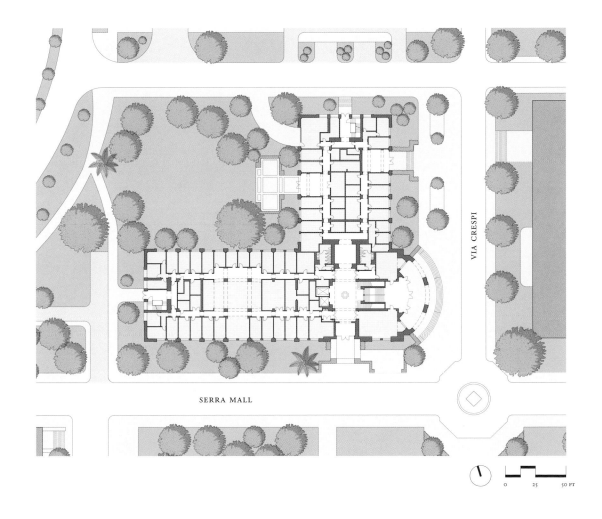

VIA CRESPI

SERRA MALL

0   25   50 FT

LEFT
Faculty lounge terrace.

RIGHT TOP
Multimedia classroom.

RIGHT BOTTOM
*Lockheed Martin
Robotics Laboratory.*

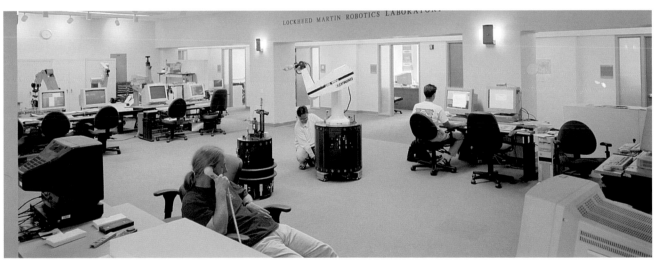

UNIVERSITY
OF CALIFORNIA,
IRVINE

IRVINE, CALIFORNIA. At 1,475 acres, the Irvine campus has only Stanford as its rival in size. Planned by William L. Pereira in 1965, conceptually it is an academical village for the automotive age, a concentric plan with principal academic structures set in a circle around a vast central park, and buildings for graduate and professional schools strung along radial streets leading to even more remote residential clusters. Rejecting the intimacy of Jefferson's academical village, Irvine is dauntingly large; the Olmsted-inspired central park has been interpreted as a monumental lawn but is in fact a largely unintelligible naturalistic landscape encircled by a mile-long pedestrian ring road.

UNIVERSITY OF CALIFORNIA, IRVINE
CAMPUS PLAN

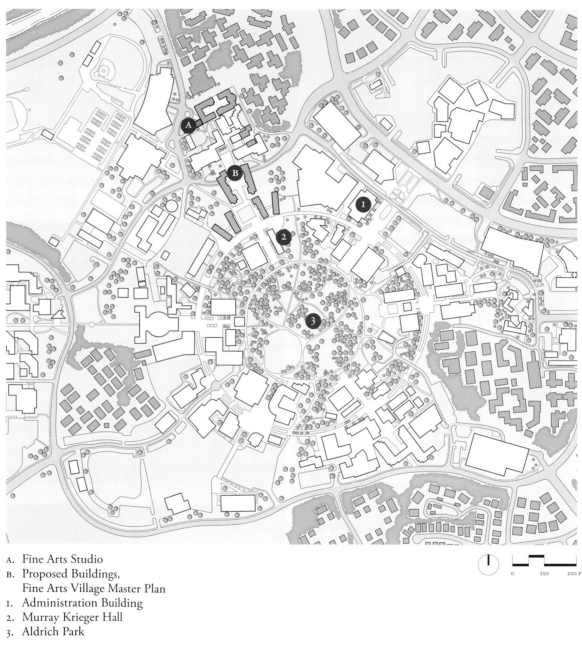

A. Fine Arts Studio
B. Proposed Buildings,
   Fine Arts Village Master Plan
1. Administration Building
2. Murray Krieger Hall
3. Aldrich Park

0   250   500 FT

STUDIO IV

1986–1989

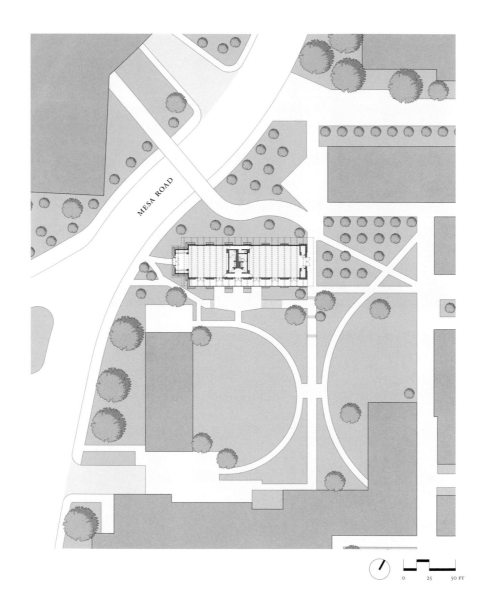

MESA ROAD

0   25   50 FT

ROBERT A.M. STERN: ON CAMPUS

COLUMBIA UNIVERSITY

NEW YORK, NEW YORK. Columbia, NYU, Johns Hopkins, Rice, and Southern Methodist confront us with new and altered iterations of the Jeffersonian paradigm, conceived for urban as opposed to rural settings.

When Columbia University was founded as King's College in 1754, it was located in a single building at what was then the outskirts of New York City on Murray Street, about one-half mile from the Battery. By 1859, the city had so closed in around the college that it moved uptown to a site in the then-outlying district near Forty-ninth Street, but bounded on one side by the steam-filled marshalling yards of two railroads, so that the ancient model of the college as a monastic cloister had a particular functional appeal.

COLUMBIA UNIVERSITY
CAMPUS PLAN

*View northeast from
Broadway and 113th Street.*

OVERLEAF
*South facade facing West
113th Street.*

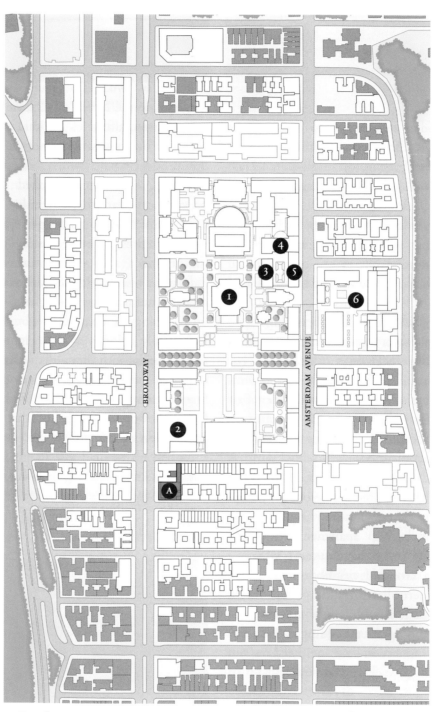

0   75   150   300 FT

A. Broadway Residence Hall
1. Low Library
2. Lerner Center
3. Avery Hall
4. Schermerhorn Hall
5. Fayerweather Hall
6. East Campus

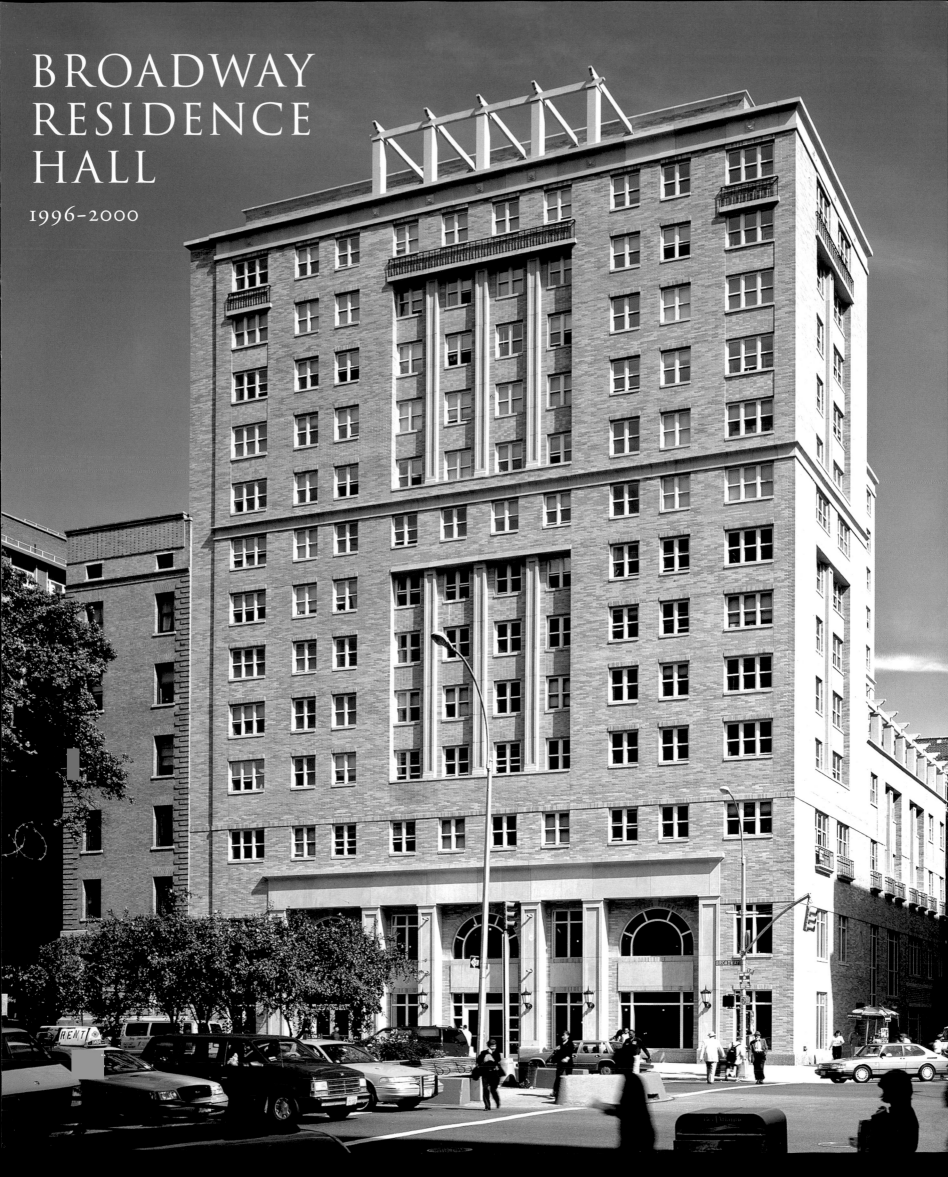

BROADWAY
RESIDENCE
HALL

1996–2000

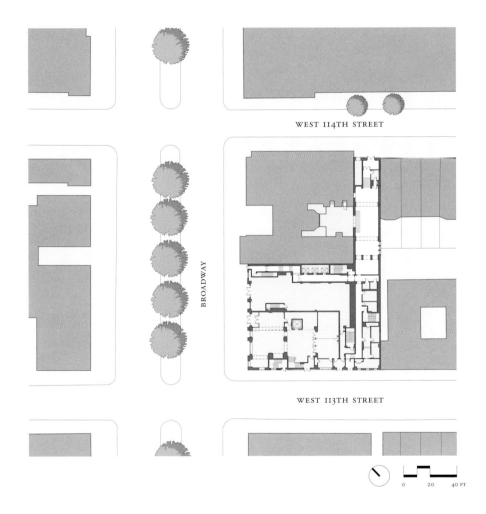

WEST 114TH STREET

BROADWAY

WEST 113TH STREET

0   20   40 FT

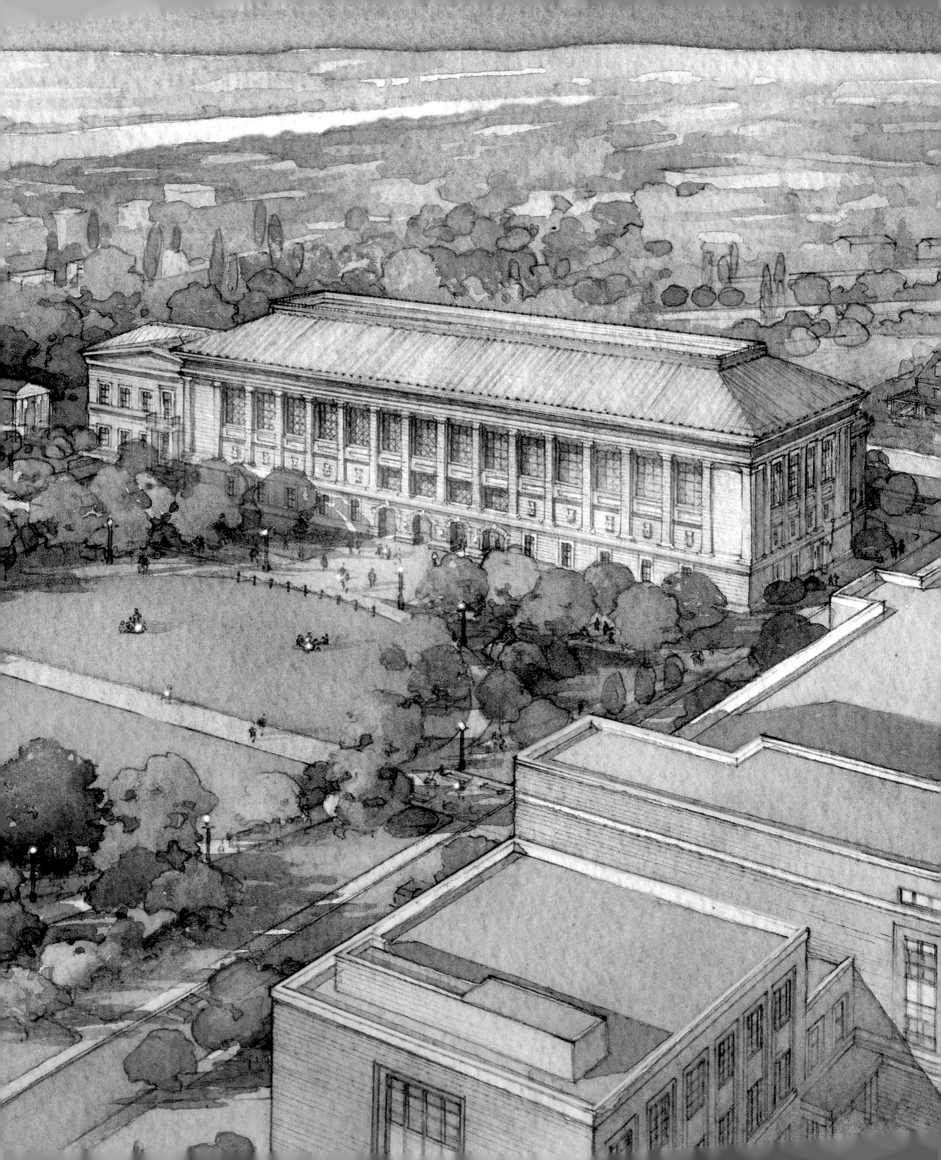

BRONX COMMUNITY COLLEGE

BRONX, NEW YORK. Six years after New York University was founded in 1831 as the University of New York City, it made its home on Manhattan Island in a single castellated Gothic building designed by Alexander Jackson Davis, set to one side of Washington Square, the city's only significant open place. When explosive urban growth threatened to engulf NYU, the university decided, following Columbia's lead, to decamp to a new campus, one even farther away from its home base.

In 1892, NYU decided to move its undergraduate college to a spectacular new fifty-acre site in the Bronx, where it commanded views of the Harlem and Hudson Rivers. While Columbia's new Morningside Heights campus, designed by Charles Follen McKim, was dismissed by Montgomery Schuyler as "pompous and expositional," "municipal" but definitely not "collegiate" in character,[1] McKim's partner, Stanford White, who was responsible for NYU's new University Heights campus, fared better, with a design in yellow brick and gray stone that Schuyler praised for its "free and vernacular use of classic forms in Georgian and Colonial work."[2] Fresh from his work restoring the Rotunda at University of Virginia and adding new buildings at the bottom of the Lawn, White developed a plan for NYU that grouped classroom buildings and dormitories around a broad green commanded at one end by a library.

Sadly, most of the buildings that were to complete White's campus were never built, and in 1956 NYU took a different approach, hiring Marcel Breuer to produce some excellent but

clashing modernist-style buildings, resulting in a competition of forms in which there could be no clear victor. Despite significant investment in the Bronx campus, NYU had never abandoned Washington Square, even though it demolished its original building in 1894. Unable to afford two campuses, the university decided to concentrate on its Manhattan

Henri Labrouste's Bibliothèque Sainte-Geneviève (1850) in Paris, a building that had inspired McKim Mead & White's Boston Public Library (1895), the North Instructional Building interacts with White's pantheonic Gould Library as Labrouste's Sainte-Geneviève complements Jacques-Germain Soufflot's Panthéon (1790). A lofty vaulted reading room promises to provide a much-needed home base on a commuter campus for students who need to get away from the hustle and bustle of the city in order to concentrate on their schoolwork.

1. Montgomery Schuyler, "Architecture of American Colleges IV—New York City Colleges," *Architectural Record* 27 (June 1910): 447, 449.
2. Schuyler, "New York City Colleges," 456.

LEFT ABOVE
North Instructional Building and Library, reading room.

LEFT BELOW
Construction view.

BELOW
Campus plan.

location and in 1973, the University Heights campus became home to Bronx Community College, which enthusiastically embraced it.

For nearly forty years, Bronx Community College did not have the opportunity to build new facilities, but a facilities assessment in 2005 triggered the decision to construct the North Instructional Building and Library. Inspired by

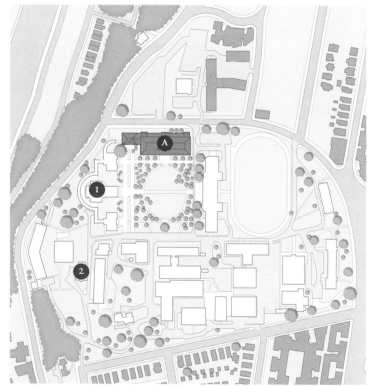

A. North Instructional Building and Library
1. Gould Library
2. Begrisch Hall

0   100   200 FT

JOHNS HOPKINS UNIVERSITY

BALTIMORE, MARYLAND. While the term "university" was used by Jefferson for the institution he founded in Virginia, in reality Harvard, Yale, Columbia, William and Mary, and the many other American institutions that established the tradition of higher education in this country were, in essence, undergraduate colleges with curricula dedicated to revealed or applied knowledge rather than to research and the discovery of new knowledge.

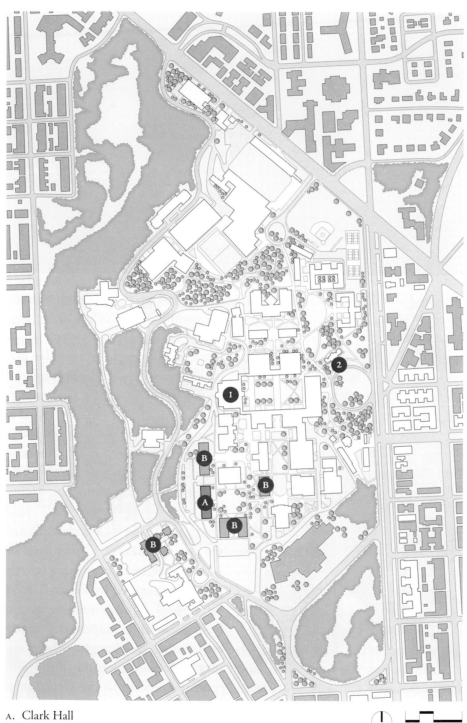

A. Clark Hall
B. Proposed Buildings, 2000 Master Plan
1. Gilman Hall
2. Homewood House

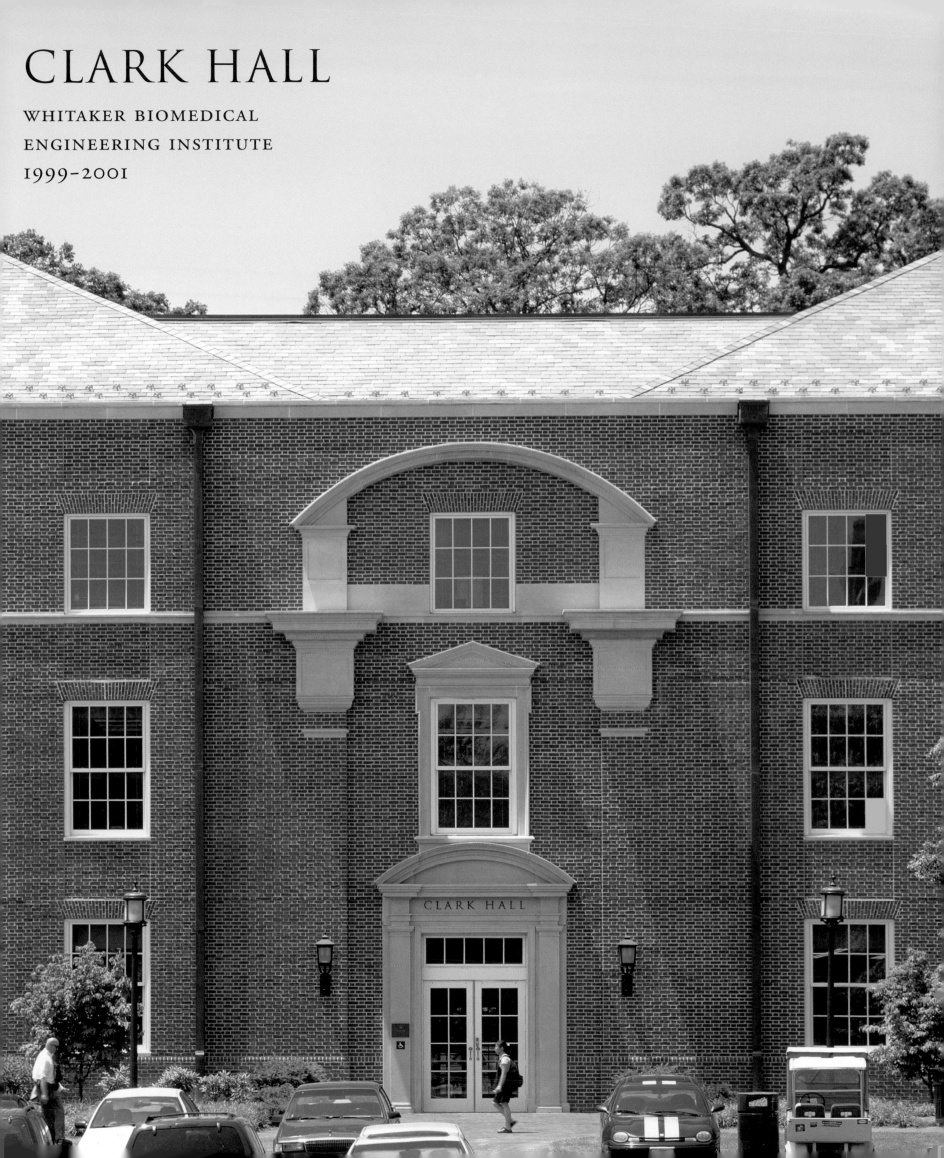

CLARK HALL

WHITAKER BIOMEDICAL
ENGINEERING INSTITUTE
1999–2001

Detail at east entry.

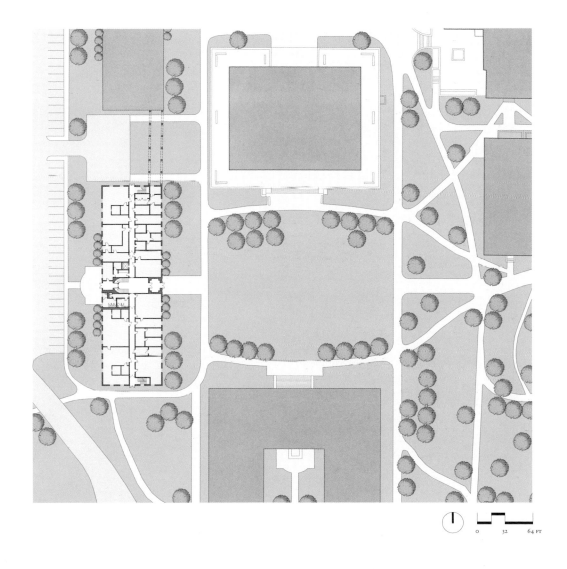

0   32   64 FT

ROBERT A.M. STERN: ON CAMPUS

East facade.

SOUTHERN METHODIST UNIVERSITY

DALLAS, TEXAS. Southern Methodist University, chartered in 1911 and located on what was initially rural prairie land north of Dallas, directly echoes the approach of Jefferson's academical village at UVA. The master plan for its initial 100-acre tract was prepared by Bremer & Pond, a Boston landscape architecture firm. Shepley, Rutan and Coolidge, also a Boston firm, whose university experience extended back to the founding of Stanford, designed SMU's first building, Dallas Hall, in 1915. This monumental, boldly pedimented Georgian-inspired copper-domed building established the palette of red brick, white columns, and white trim that continues to prevail.

SOUTHERN METHODIST UNIVERSITY
CAMPUS PLAN

A. George W. Bush Presidential Center
1. Dallas Hall
2. McFarlin Auditorium

GEORGE W. BUSH
PRESIDENTIAL CENTER

2007–

LEFT TOP
West facade with entrance to the Institute.

LEFT BOTTOM
View from southwest.

OVERLEAF
Entrance to the Institute from Binkley Avenue.

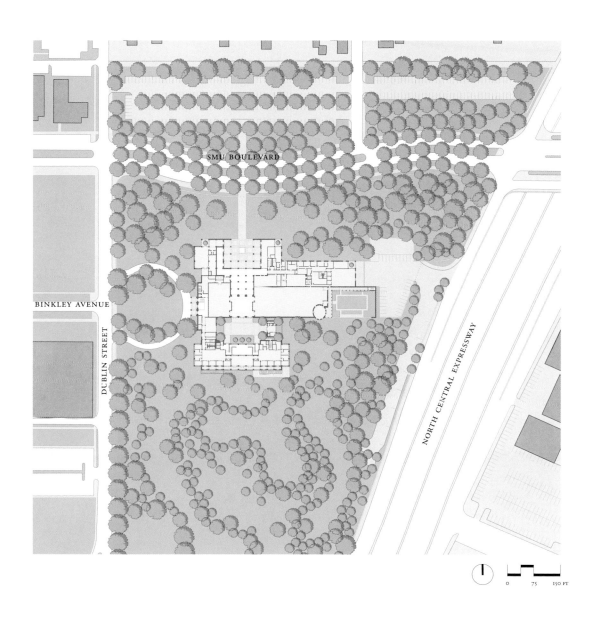

SMU BOULEVARD

BINKLEY AVENUE

DUBLIN STREET

NORTH CENTRAL EXPRESSWAY

0   75   150 FT

UNIVERSITY OF NEBRASKA

LINCOLN, NEBRASKA. The University of Nebraska has two campuses: the original City Campus, downtown, and "The Farm" or East Campus, approximately two miles to the northeast, where grandly proportioned buff brick buildings of the Beaux-Arts era bump up against abundant landscape and a confusing post–World War II era mélange.

INTERNATIONAL QUILT STUDY CENTER AND MUSEUM

2004–2008

LEFT
Reception hall.

RIGHT TOP
Reception hall.

RIGHT BOTTOM
Galleries.

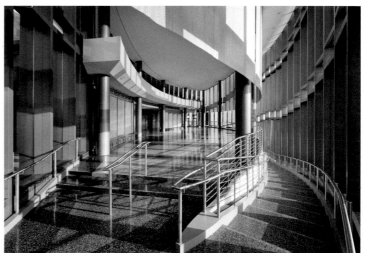

RICE UNIVERSITY

HOUSTON, TEXAS. The extraordinary power of coherent campus design to propel new colleges and universities into leadership positions, as exemplified by Stanford University, inspired many faltering institutions to seriously consider the issue of physical planning and architectural expression as part of their strategic planning. By the early 1900s, Columbia, New York University, and Johns Hopkins had relocated to new planned campuses, soon to be followed by the Rice Institute, a polytechnic school founded in 1859.

McNAIR HALL

JONES GRADUATE SCHOOL OF BUSINESS

1999–2002

PREVIOUS PAGES
View from northeast.

BELOW
*South facade from Jamail
Plaza.*

OVERLEAF
South facade at main entry.

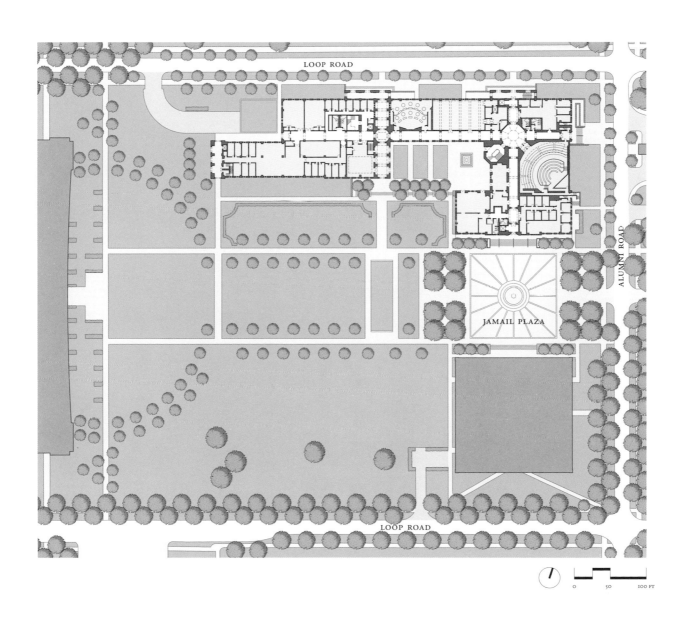

LOOP ROAD

ALUMNI ROAD

JAMAIL PLAZA

LOOP ROAD

0   50   100 FT

LEFT
Main entrance with bull and bear sculptures, doors, and overdoor by Kent Bloomer.

RIGHT
Woodson Courtyard looking east.

OVERLEAF
Library.

LEFT
Main stair.

RIGHT TOP
*Shell Oil Foundation
Auditorium.*

RIGHT BOTTOM
Boardroom in dean's suite.

INDIANA UNIVERSITY PURDUE UNIVERSITY

INDIANAPOLIS, INDIANA. The modernist architect Edward Larrabee Barnes held Jefferson's academical village in high regard, using it as a model for the 500-acre campus designed in 1976 to accommodate the merged Indianapolis branches of Indiana and Purdue Universities. Regrettably, Barnes's own buildings did not serve this vision as well as they could have and subsequent construction by others rendered the campus chaotic.

INFORMATICS AND
COMMUNICATIONS
TECHNOLOGY
COMPLEX

1998–2003

PREVIOUS PAGES
*West facade from
quadrangle.*

LEFT
*Corner towers along
North West Street*

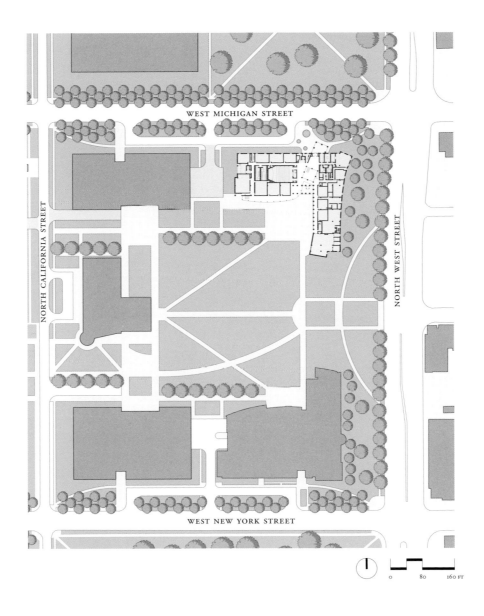

WEST MICHIGAN STREET

NORTH CALIFORNIA STREET

NORTH WEST STREET

WEST NEW YORK STREET

0   80   160 FT

LEFT
Atrium.

RIGHT TOP
Lounge.

RIGHT BOTTOM
Gallery.

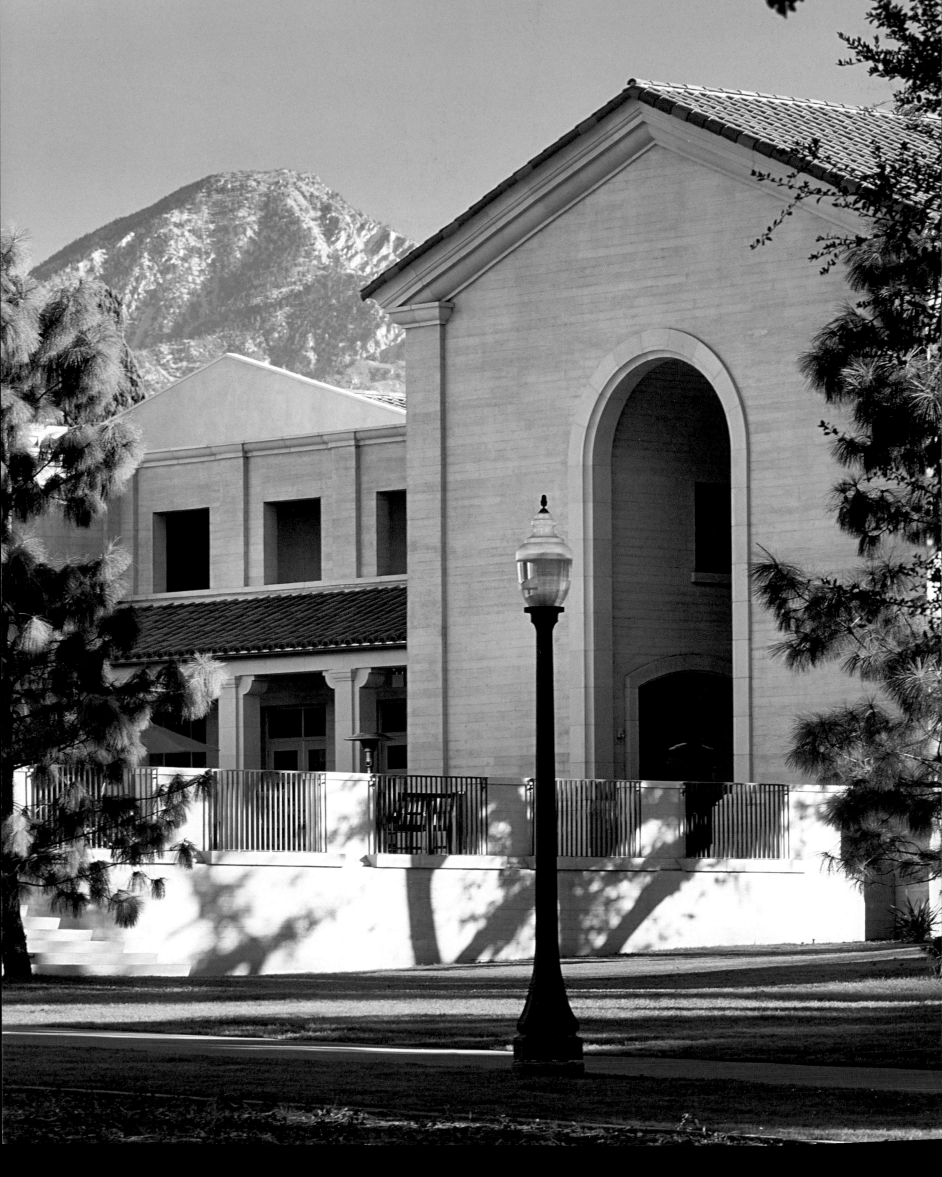

POMONA COLLEGE

CLAREMONT, CALIFORNIA. The campus of Pomona College, though constituting one of the most interesting interpretations of Jefferson's plan for the University of Virginia, is significantly different in one respect: unlike the campus at Charlottesville, which was planned as its own self-contained village, Pomona College was firmly embedded in the town of Claremont, California; in fact, it may be said more accurately that Pomona College gave Claremont its reason for being. As is the case with so much that is artistically and urbanistically distinguished in man-made America, Pomona's campus development combines lofty ideals with the hard-boiled pragmatism of a real estate deal.

SMITH CAMPUS CENTER

1993–1999

PREVIOUS PAGES
View from southeast.

BELOW
*Aerial view looking
northwest.*

OVERLEAF
Courtyard looking west.

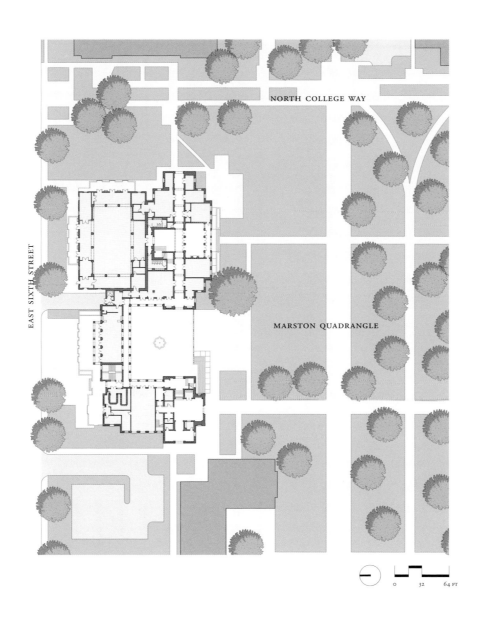

NORTH COLLEGE WAY

EAST SIXTH STREET

MARSTON QUADRANGLE

0   32   64 FT

FAR LEFT
Open-air gallery.

LEFT
West entrance to open-air gallery.

RIGHT
Open-air stair.

UNIVERSITY OF NOTRE DAME

NOTRE DAME, INDIANA. Founded by French missionaries in 1842, the University of Notre Dame quickly grew into a major institution, with a campus organized around a large quadrangle dominated by the campus's first focal structure, not a church but an administration building, which burned and was replaced by an imposing gold-domed building (1879) designed by Willoughby J. Edbrooke, a Chicago architect best known for monumental public edifices. Edbrooke described the Main Building as "modern gothic,"[1] though it has more accurately been characterized as "an eclectic and somewhat naïve combination of pointed windows, medieval moldings and classical columns."[2]

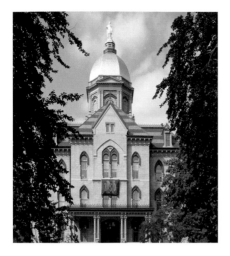

After the construction of the Basilica of the Sacred Heart, in Gothic style in the 1870s and 1880s, and the Main Building's reconstruction in 1879, the campus grew southward and eastward, so that the original quad, which has come to be known as the "God Quad," though framed by the two buildings most associated with the architectural identity of the university, no longer constitutes its geographic center.

In 1920, Francis Kervick, head of the university's architecture department, developed a grand Jeffersonian mall comparable in size to six football fields. Despite its vastness, Kervick believed the mall would foster "that sequestered peace one feels on the common of an early American village."[3] Along with Professor Vincent Fagan, Kervick designed the first three buildings on this axis in the Collegiate Gothic style, establishing the architectural vocabulary that would be reaffirmed by Ralph Adams Cram, who, after receiving an honorary degree from the university in 1924, expressed his interest in contributing to the institution's physical plant. Beginning with South Dining Hall (1927), Cram and his successor firm, McGinnis and Walsh, filled out the edges of the quad with simple, quiet Gothic buildings executed in buff brick, stone accents, and sloped slate roofs, allowing the Main Building and the Basilica to maintain their prominence.

Between 1952 and 1976 Notre Dame's campus expanded southward and eastward, spurred along by the Ellerbe and Associates 1967 master plan, which mapped out DeBartolo Quadrangle, forming an increasingly important new campus entry. Near the quadrangle's east end lies the site of our Stayer Center for Executive Education, a freestanding component of Notre Dame's Mendoza College of Business. Carrying forward the architectural tradition established by Cram with the Notre Dame brick blend specific to the campus, cast stone trim and string

courses, and slate, Stayer's H-shaped plan will define two landscaped terraces, one of which will form a courtyard when a future interlocking U-shaped building is built to the south, completing the long eastern edge of DeBartolo Quad. Though remote from the original center of the campus, Stayer's upper-floor social room will offer views to Main's golden dome.

1. Willoughby Edbrooke quoted in Damaine Vonada, *Notre Dame: The Official Campus Guide* (Notre Dame, Ind.: University of Notre Dame Press, 1998), 20.
2. Francis Kervick, quoted in Thomas J. Schlereth, *The University of Notre Dame: A Portrait of Its History and Campus* (Notre Dame, Ind.: University of Notre Dame Press, 1976), 58.
3. Kervick quoted in Vonada, 93.

UNIVERSITY OF NOTRE DAME
CAMPUS PLAN

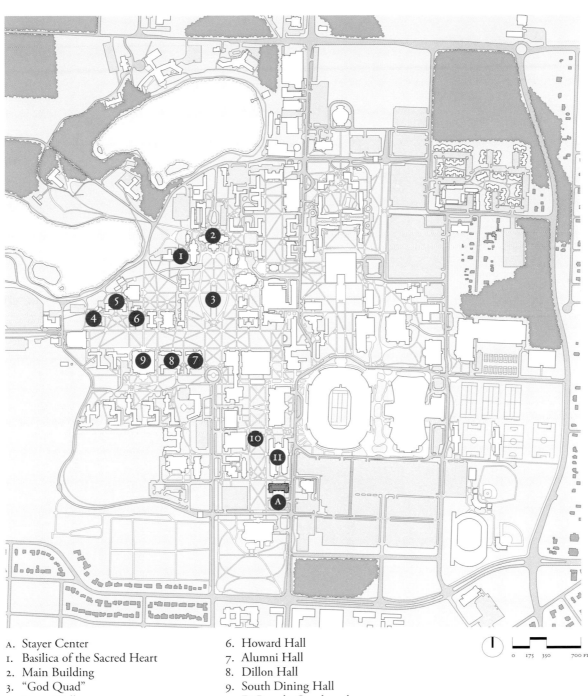

A. Stayer Center
1. Basilica of the Sacred Heart
2. Main Building
3. "God Quad"
4. Lyons Hall
5. Morrissey Hall
6. Howard Hall
7. Alumni Hall
8. Dillon Hall
9. South Dining Hall
10. DeBartolo Quadrangle
11. Mendoza College of Business

0   175   350   700 FT

FRANKLIN & MARSHALL COLLEGE

LANCASTER, PENNSYLVANIA. When Franklin College, founded in 1787, and Marshall College, founded in 1836, combined to form Franklin & Marshall College in 1853, the leaders of the merged institution chose a ten-acre site to the northwest of Lancaster, Pennsylvania, and turned to the Baltimore-based architects Dixon, Balbirnie and Dixon, a firm known for its work in the Greek and Gothic revival styles, for three Gothic buildings completed in 1856–57: College Building, now called Old Main, flanked by Diagnothian and Goethean Halls.

ABOVE
Master plan, Charles Z. Klauder, 1925.

RIGHT
Northwest quadrant plan, Robert A. M. Stern Architects, 2008.

In the latter half of the nineteenth century, the campus grew with buildings designed by an eclectic group of architects in a variety of styles, until 1923 when Charles Z. Klauder, a Philadelphia-based architect specializing in collegiate planning and architecture, was retained as campus architect.

Klauder was one of the nation's most prolific architects of academic buildings. It is no exaggeration to say he wrote the book on the subject: his comprehensive and influential *College Architecture in America* (with Herbert C. Wise, 1929) was the first important compendium of its kind, and in many ways an inspiration for this volume. Klauder mastered a variety of styles: Gothic at Princeton, Yale, and St. Paul's School; red-brick Georgian at the University of Delaware, in a plan explicitly based on Jefferson's University of Virginia; and even new vocabularies of his own devising, as at the University of Colorado at Boulder. At Franklin & Marshall, Klauder worked in the Georgian style, contributing his ideas first to a new gymnasium by another architect, William C. Pritchett, and then to two dormitories, which he used to establish an architectural vocabulary appropriate to a college that, though squarely rooted in the history of the early republic, had not yet found its physical identity. Klauder's master plan for the campus

created quadrangles set along cardinal axes framed by bar-shaped buildings, with his own Hensel Hall (1927) at its heart. By 1931 he had dramatically transformed an aesthetic jumble into a cohesive place.

The structure of Klauder's plan governed college construction through the remainder of the twentieth century, even as buildings of varying quality filled in available sites. A 2008 master plan by Ayers Saint Gross proposed a new formal entrance to the college intended to improve its presence on Harrisburg Pike and integrate the campus with newly acquired real estate slated for use as the college's recreational precinct. Our contribution to the Franklin & Marshall campus began with a plan for its northwest quadrant, with future buildings proposed to enclose a new quadrangle and address the intersection of Harrisburg Pike and Race Avenue. The first of those buildings, New College House, now under construction, will accommodate two hundred students in a variety of room types including suites and apartments organized to support a sense of shared domesticity. Slate roofs crown a composition of simple stone-trimmed red brick pavilions, carrying forward the heritage of Klauder's beloved Georgian.

FRANKLIN & MARSHALL COLLEGE
CAMPUS PLAN

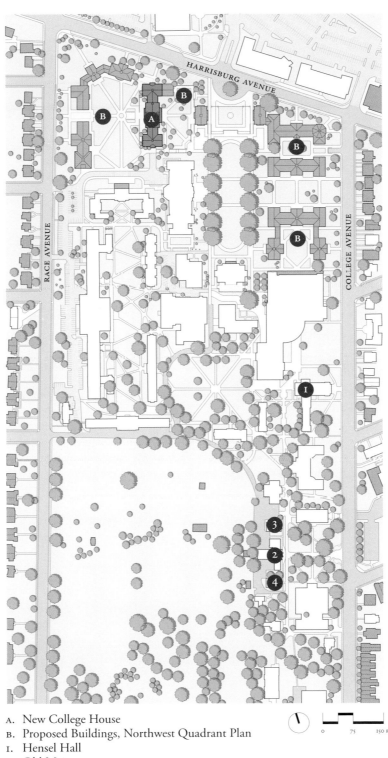

A. New College House
B. Proposed Buildings, Northwest Quadrant Plan
1. Hensel Hall
2. Old Main
3. Diagnothian Hall
4. Goethean Hall

THE HOTCHKISS SCHOOL

LAKEVILLE, CONNECTICUT. The Hotchkiss School was founded in 1891 by Maria Bissell Hotchkiss, a former schoolteacher and heir to the immense fortune bequeathed her by her estranged husband, Benjamin Berkeley Hotchkiss, who worked in the family business of developing weapons and military hardware. Hotchkiss's initial impulse to found a school to educate developmentally challenged children was redirected by Timothy Dwight, then president of Yale University, towards the establishment of a boarding school where young men of promise, including deserving boys from impoverished local families, would be prepared for entrance to Yale.

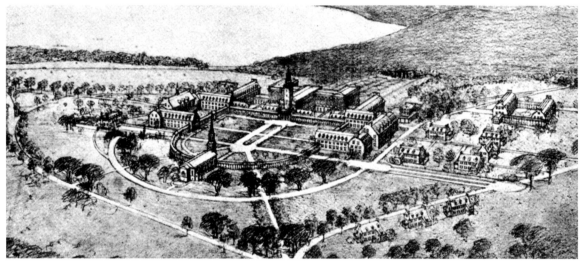

Unlike many of the other new boarding schools of the time, such as Taft, that made do with re-purposed buildings until they could establish campuses of their own, Maria Hotchkiss's gift of land and funds allowed her school to establish its architectural identity all at once.

Responsibility for the school's original buildings went to Bruce Price, a New York architect known for office buildings in Manhattan,

houses in Tuxedo Park, and Canadian railroad hotels including the Chateau Frontenac in Quebec, as well as two buildings at Yale. For Hotchkiss, Price designed a single Main Building for administration (1892), attached by means of a wide, one-story corridor to flanking buildings containing the academic teaching spaces and the peripheral programs vital to the boys' time at the school—a gymnasium, a chapel, and a dining hall. Student residence halls were located in separate buildings. Although Price's complex crowned a hill like a citadel, its arrangement of pavilions strung along a corridor distinctly reflects Jeffersonian precedent.

As the campus grew from its original 65 acres to the 550 it now enjoys, Main continued to function as the school's academic heart, but additional freestanding buildings, mostly dormitories, were built to meet the school's growth. In the 1920s, Cass Gilbert, another important New York architect, best known for his Custom House at Bowling Green and the Woolworth

estates and club houses such as the Knickerbocker and Colony Clubs in New York. Of the three architects who formed the Hotchkiss campus over its first fifty years, William Adams Delano had the most impact, developing a master plan that was adopted, adding two dormitories, a dining hall, a chapel, entrance gates and a library and, on a site across the road, a gymnasium, all in all exhibiting "the possibilities of brick as an ornamental feature."[1]

Building in New York, but also well regarded for his university campus plans for Minnesota and Texas universities, proposed monumental, open green spaces and quadrangles, bounded by a semicircular campus-defining road. Gilbert's plan was ignored, but he designed three buildings, all freestanding dormitories. While Price's designs were based on American Georgian, his approach to his sources was eclectic rather than scholarly. Gilbert introduced a scholarly tradition, substituting red brick for the pale yellow brick Price preferred.

Gilbert was succeeded by the New York firm of Delano & Aldrich, best known for country

In the 1960s, although red brick remained the preferred building material, architects retained by the school strayed from the Georgian tradition. Paul Rudolph's proposal for a "New Main" (1964) was not realized, but a version by Hugh Stubbins (1967) so compromised the campus character that it was quickly modified by Evans Woollen and completely camouflaged by Shope Reno Wharton in 1995.

Despite some recent academic buildings in modernist styles, Hotchkiss has re-embraced the Georgian as a result of a new master plan by Butler Rogers Baskett Architects, leading to the construction of our Edelman and Flinn

ABOVE
Bissell Hall, Bruce Price, 1894.

BELOW LEFT
Edsel Ford Memorial Library, Delano & Aldrich, 1952.

BELOW RIGHT
Chapel, Delano & Aldrich, 1931.

ABOVE
*Main Building, Shope
Reno Wharton, 1995.*

RIGHT
*Main Building, Evans
Wollen, 1983.*

BELOW
*Main Building, Hugh
Stubbins, 1967.*

residential halls (2009) which, together with
Bissell Hall, the last remaining of Price's buildings, define a new quadrangle. Edelman and
Flinn each consist of a central gabled block
housing student rooms, bookended by gam-
brel-roofed side dependencies accommodating
faculty apartments. Similar in size and in their
shared Georgian vocabulary to the dormitories
designed by Gilbert and Delano, Edelman and
Flinn are fraternal rather than identical twins,
both massed in red brick punctuated by dou-
ble-hung shuttered windows, but with Ionic
detailing at Edelman and Doric at Flinn.

1. Peter Pennoyer and Anne Walker, *The Architecture of Delano &
Aldrich* (New York and London: W.W. Norton, 2003), 59–60.

THE HOTCHKISS SCHOOL
CAMPUS PLAN

A. Flinn Hall
B. Edelman Hall
1. Main Building
2. Chapel
3. Edsel Ford Memorial Library
4. Bissell Hall

0   100   200 FT

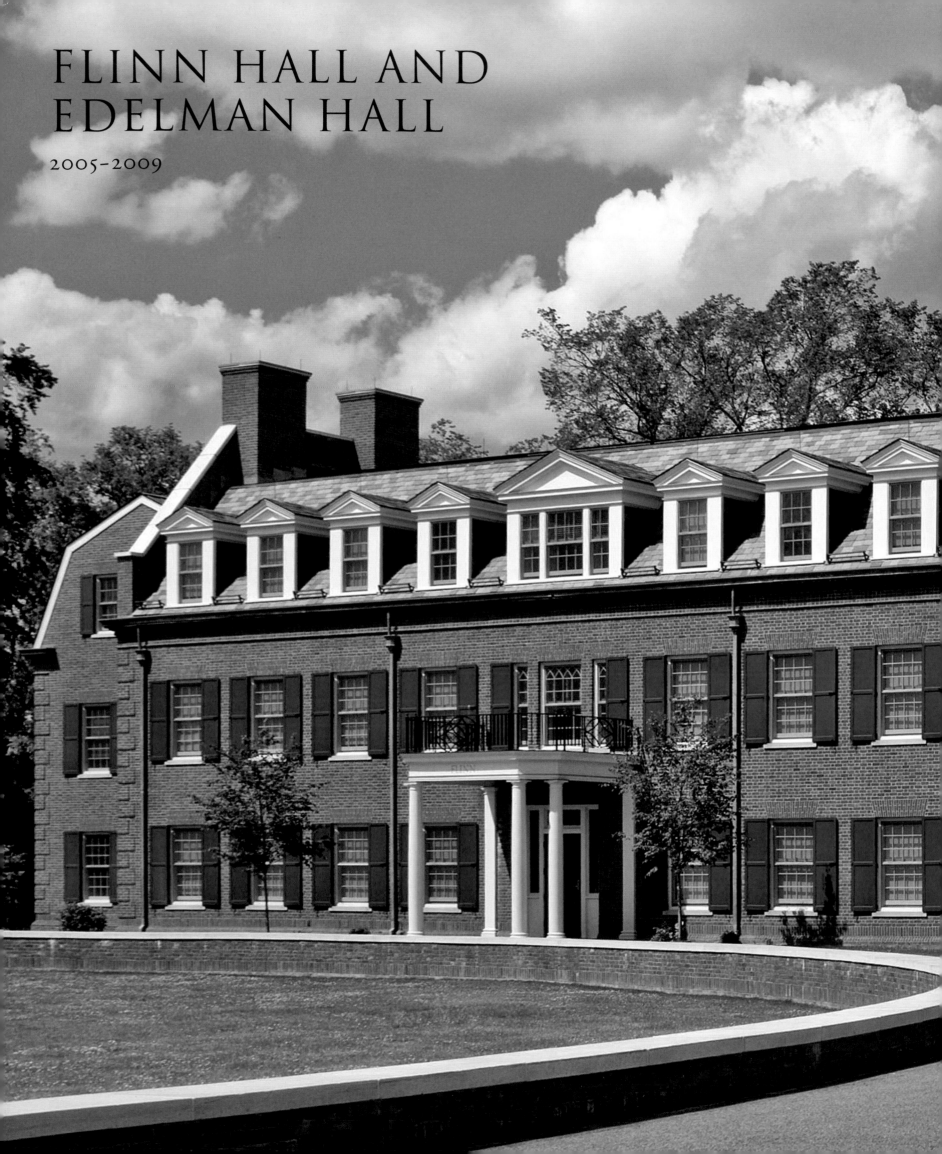

FLINN HALL AND
EDELMAN HALL

2005–2009

PREVIOUS PAGES
*View looking northeast
to Flinn Hall.*

RIGHT
*West entrance to
Edelman Hall.*

OVERLEAF
*View looking northeast
across new quadrangle.*

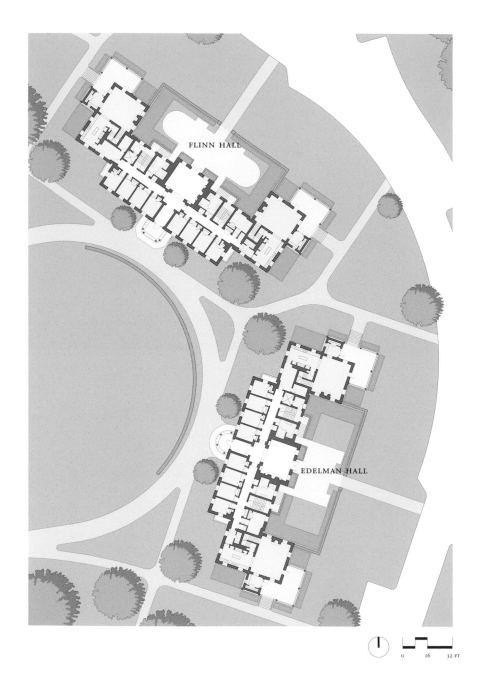

FLINN HALL

EDELMAN HALL

0   16   32 FT

LEFT
North court at Flinn Hall.

RIGHT
*Porch at faculty wing of
Flinn Hall.*

LEFT TOP
Student commons.

LEFT BOTTOM
Faculty apartment.

RIGHT TOP
Upper-floor lounge.

RIGHT BOTTOM
Student bedroom

UNIVERSITY OF COLORADO AT BOULDER

BOULDER, COLORADO. Set in the foothills of the Rockies, the University of Colorado at Boulder is a rare twentieth-century example of a new campus perfectly attuned to its setting. Such was not always the case. Colorado's early buildings were many and varied versions of prevailing trends and fashions, leading George Norlin, the university's president from 1919 to 1939, to observe that the place looked like a "third-rate farm."[1] Norlin turned to the architect Charles Z. Klauder, who first proposed a version of the Collegiate Gothic style, but after careful consideration of the site, changed directions and went on to propose a central court surrounded by stone buildings capped by low-pitched red-tile roofs.

Klauder refused to apply a stylistic label to his work, which has been described as "Rural Italian" and "Tuscan Vernacular," but in 1934, in reply to President Norlin's asking whether what had been built constituted "a University of Colorado style of architecture," he stated that

the style of the building is a combination of elements found elsewhere, cast by an inventive hand into a new harmony and thus acquiring originality and individuality. This has always taken place when that which has character in an old style is made into a living one.[2]

Klauder died in 1938 and his successor firm continued to build in the Colorado manner, but with somewhat less conviction. In 1963, at the height of International Style modernism's popularity, and with one of its great institutional ensembles, Skidmore, Owings & Merrill's spectacular Air Force Academy, being realized just a short distance away, the landscape architect Hideo Sasaki and the architect Pietro Belluschi countered prevailing trends with a new master plan that dramatically resisted the temptation to go "modern."

In 2008 we were asked to develop a master plan for the university's new East Campus designed for the sciences. Reflecting Klauder's approach

and Sasaki's embellishments but at the larger scale that is required for twenty-first-century academic laboratory buildings, the 260,000-square-foot pavilionated Caruthers Systems Biotechnology Building, to be completed in 2011, will be the first building realized as part of our plan. Holding down one side of what will be a quadrangle, the Caruthers pavilions organize labs and faculty offices into neighborhoods, encouraging collegial interaction, that open onto a central "main street" lined with shared support spaces and meeting rooms.

As Klauder's did, our campus plan and building design work with the natural landscape, prevailing winds, and solar orientation—labs face north and south to allow for maximum control over daylight and to offer spectacular views to the Flatirons, the front range of the Rockies. The palette of local sandstone, brick, and red barrel-tile roofs echoes Klauder's buildings, but is sufficiently different in detail to establish a distinct identity for the East Campus.

1. George Norlin quoted in William R. Deno, *Body and Soul: Architectural Style at the University of Colorado at Boulder* (Boulder: University of Colorado at Boulder Publications Service, 1994), 2, n. 3.
2. George Norlin and Charles Z. Klauder quoted in Claire Shepherd Lanier, *Contextual Eclecticism: Designing Distinctive Campus Architecture for the University of Colorado, 1917-1921,* (Denver, Co.: University of Colorado, 2005), 108-9.

TOP
Reed Hall, Charles Z. Klauder, 1929.

ABOVE
Norlin Library, Charles Z. Klauder, 1940.

BELOW
Master plan, Charles Z. Klauder, 1919.

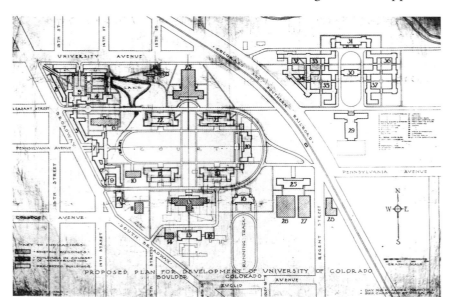

UNIVERSITY OF
COLORADO AT BOULDER
CAMPUS PLAN

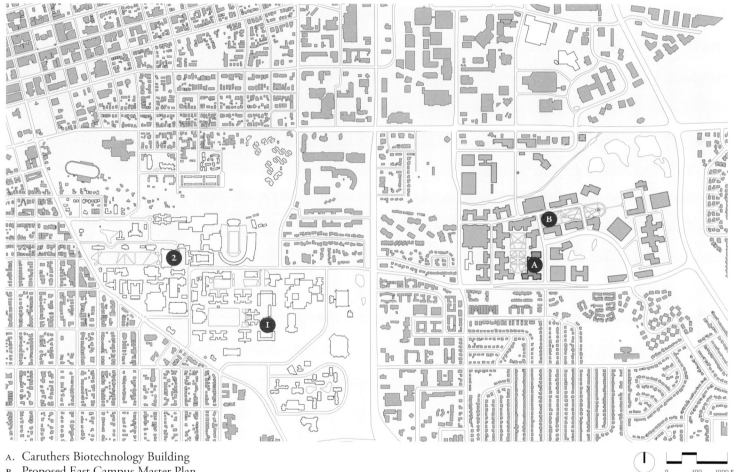

A. Caruthers Biotechnology Building
B. Proposed East Campus Master Plan
1. Reed Hall
2. Norlin Library

0   500   1000 FT

FLORIDA INTERNATIONAL UNIVERSITY

MIAMI, FLORIDA. Florida International University, founded in 1965, occupies the site of a former airport. FIU is a very new place and typical of post-Vietnam-era dystopianism with no strong sense of architecture in the service of a shared ideal. Architecturally, it is like a child just learning to speak. There is an outpouring of words but little grammar to bind them together into coherent thought, with the spaces between the buildings as barely formed as a child's sentences.

DIAZ-BALART HALL

FIU COLLEGE OF LAW
2002–2006

PREVIOUS PAGES
*Main entry from Avenue
of the Professions.*

LEFT
*Balcony off main reading
room.*

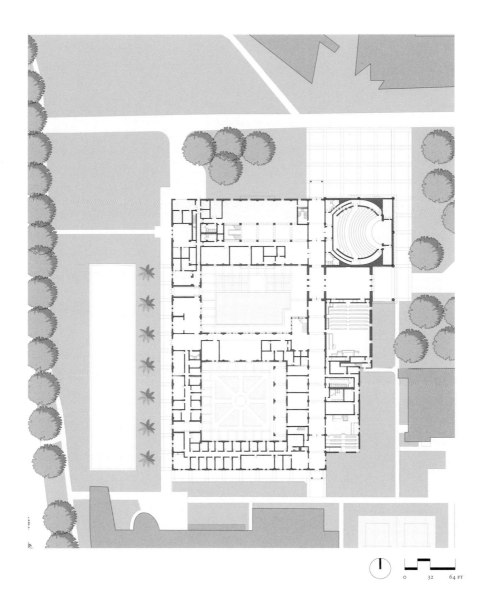

0   32   64 FT

LEFT TOP
North courtyard.

LEFT BOTTOM
South courtyard.

RIGHT
Lobby.

FLORIDA SOUTHERN COLLEGE

LAKELAND, FLORIDA. Frank Lloyd Wright cast himself as heir to Thomas Jefferson's vision, but had still higher ambitions, so it is fitting that this section devoted to Jefferson's impact concludes with Wright's work at Florida Southern College (1938–58). Jefferson's architecture had its basis in historic precedent, but Wright wanted to formulate a new language that he believed would even more accurately reflect the self-invention of our American democracy. Wright got his only chance to realize his über-Jeffersonian vision at the scale of a campus at Florida Southern College.

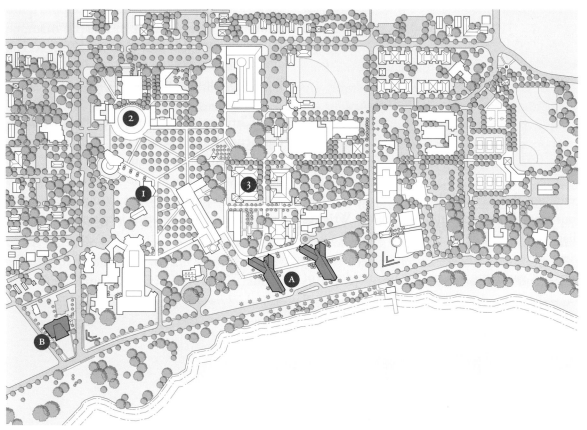

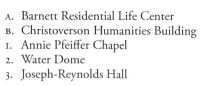

A. Barnett Residential Life Center
B. Christoverson Humanities Building
1. Annie Pfeiffer Chapel
2. Water Dome
3. Joseph-Reynolds Hall

0   75   150   300 FT

BARNETT
RESIDENTIAL
LIFE CENTER

2005–2009

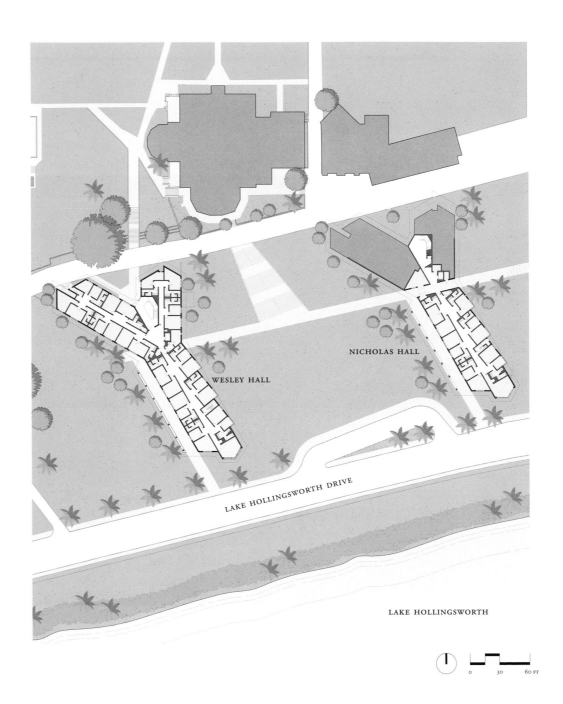

NICHOLAS HALL

WESLEY HALL

LAKE HOLLINGSWORTH DRIVE

LAKE HOLLINGSWORTH

0   30   60 FT

LEFT
Third-floor lounge.

RIGHT TOP
Fourth-floor lounge.

RIGHT BOTTOM
Stair.

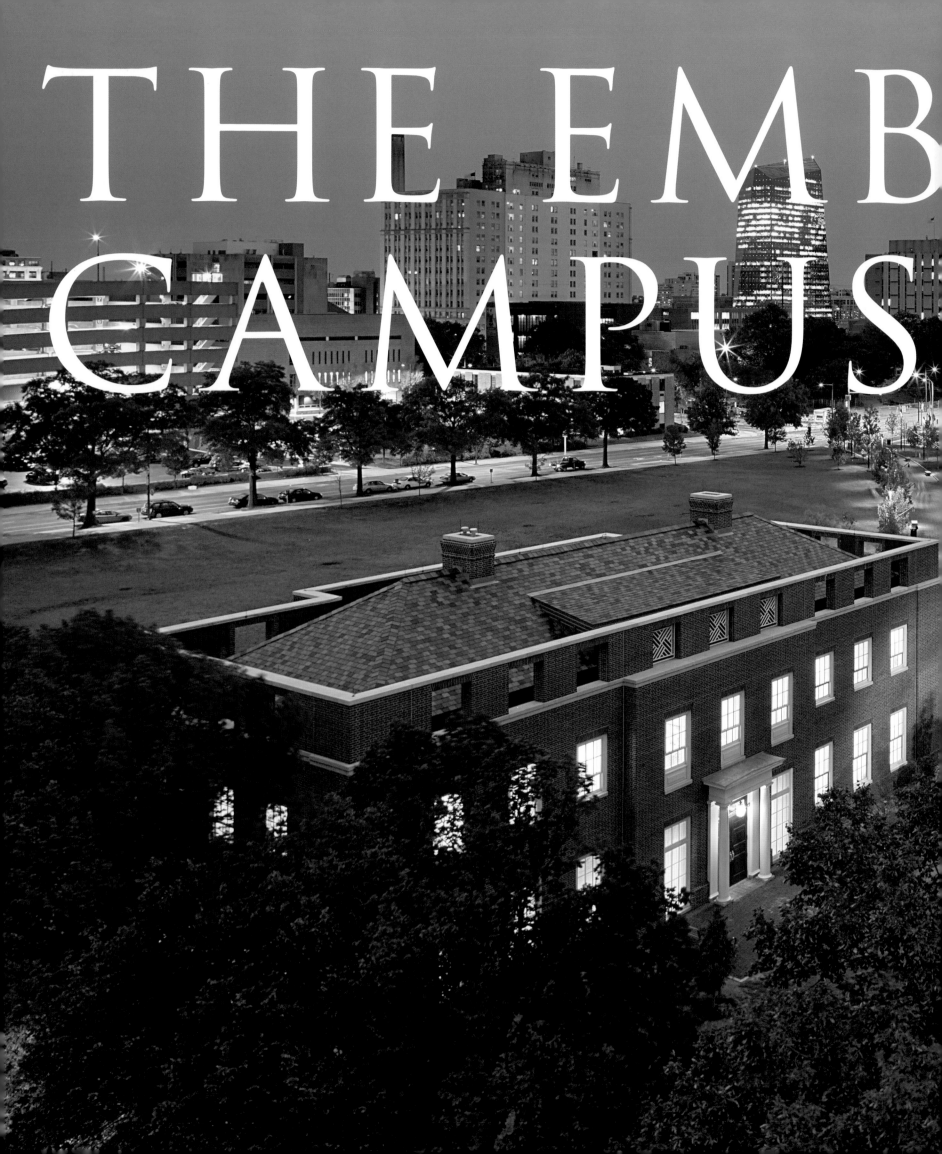

THE EMB
CAMPUS

SOME OF THE MOST RESPECTED AMERICAN campuses are neither holistically conceived villages, nor gardenesque arcadias, nor hilltop citadels, but groups of buildings embedded in a town.

Although inextricably connected to their urban settings, embedded campuses are not indistinguishable from them, as the Sorbonne is from Paris. Instead, as is the case with the various colleges and buildings that comprise Oxford and Cambridge Universities, the components of embedded campuses are readily identified by gates or walls or moats, by the size and character of the architecture of their buildings, and by planning configurations, frequently taking the form of cloisters and closed quadrangles.

PAGES 248–249
*The McNeil Center for
Early American Studies,
University of Pennsylvania.*

LEFT
Spangler Campus Center.

HARVARD UNIVERSITY

CAMBRIDGE, MASSACHUSETTS. Harvard University, founded in 1636, sprawls across two cities, Cambridge and Boston, possessing, as Neil Rudenstine, its president between 1991 and 2001, has written, "a number of identifiable precincts where several of the features of a campus are predominant," but lack a unified identity, constituting "interludes" that "tend to be episodic."[1] Harvard began in Cambridge with a building that looked like a modest house in Elizabethan England. Only as the college expanded in the eighteenth century did it establish a campus—the Yard—slowly filling it up with straightforward red brick Georgian-style buildings of no particular pretensions until Charles Bulfinch provided a focal point, the white-granite University Hall (1815).

SPANGLER CAMPUS CENTER

HARVARD BUSINESS SCHOOL
1997–2001

PREVIOUS PAGES
*North facade facing
Aldrich Hall.*

LEFT
*Entrance on Gordon
Circle.*

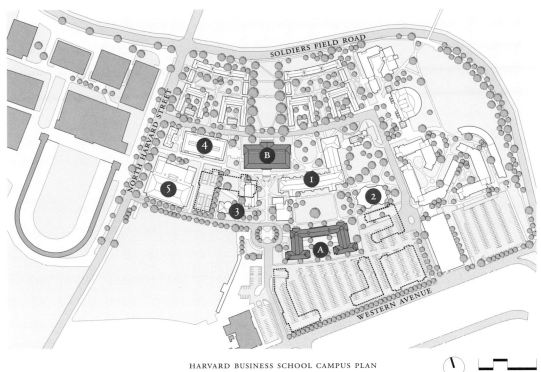

HARVARD BUSINESS SCHOOL CAMPUS PLAN

A. Spangler Campus Center
B. Baker Library |
   Bloomberg Center
1. Aldrich Hall

2. Burden Hall
3. Chapel
4. Morgan Hall
5. Shad Field House

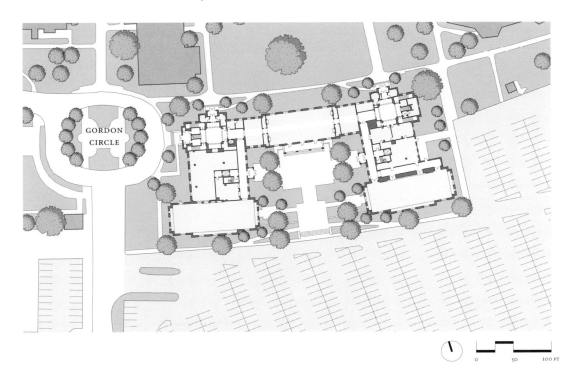

LEFT
*Entrance rotunda
and stair hall.*

RIGHT
Servery.

OVERLEAF
Dining hall.

BAKER LIBRARY |
BLOOMBERG CENTER

HARVARD BUSINESS SCHOOL

2002–2005

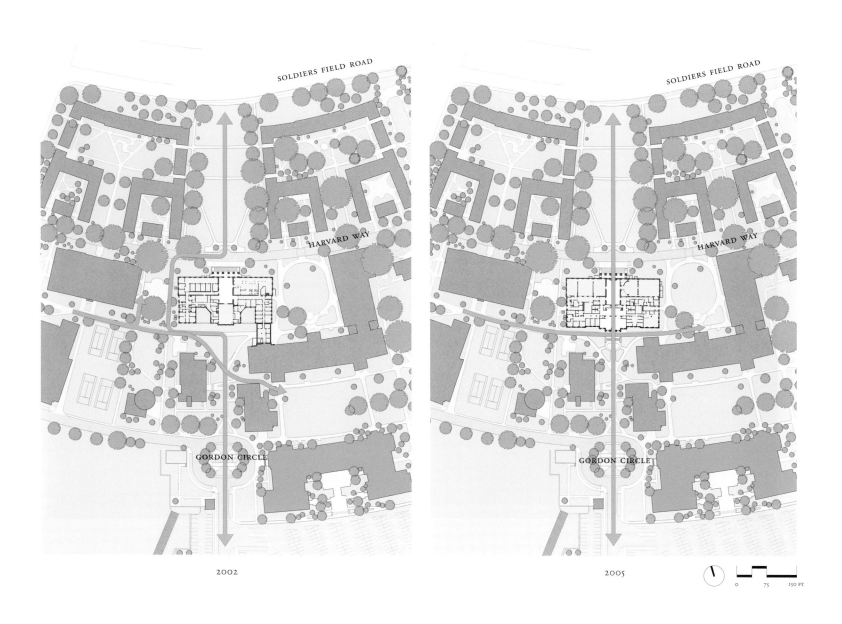

SOLDIERS FIELD ROAD

HARVARD WAY

GORDON CIRCLE

2002

SOLDIERS FIELD ROAD

HARVARD WAY

GORDON CIRCLE

2005

0   75   150 FT

WASSERSTEIN HALL, CASPERSEN STUDENT CENTER, AND CLINICAL WING

HARVARD LAW SCHOOL

2004–2011

Tower of north residential
college from Farmington
Canal Trail.

YALE UNIVERSITY

NEW HAVEN, CONNECTICUT. Yale's campus is even more deeply embedded in its host city than Harvard's. Founded in 1701 in Saybrook, Connecticut, by Congregational ministers, Yale relocated in 1717 to New Haven, where it initially occupied one of the nine squares of the city's ideal plan and now occupies one-and-one-half more of those squares as well as considerable other properties extending to the north and south to form a two-and-one-half mile, virtually unbroken spine of institutional ownership threaded through the town.

By 1782 Yale had grown so much that its original building was removed to make way for College Row, an alternating arrangement of red brick Georgian-style dormitories and meeting halls. With painter John Trumbull acting as informal aesthetic adviser, College Row was in essence the first example of an American campus deliberately planned to meet both functional and aesthetic criteria in an urban ensemble. Unlike at Harvard, where the buildings of the Yard faced away from the street, Yale's College Row opened to the city, addressing the public green that formed the central square of New Haven's nine-square plan from behind small, symmetrical front yards, bordered by a low wood fence. In the back, beyond the privies, Trumbull planted a picturesque English garden.

Charles Dickens in his *American Notes* (1842) admired the still-Georgian campus:

The various departments . . . are erected in a kind of park or common in the middle of the town, where they are dimly visible among the shadowing trees. The effect is very like that of an old cathedral yard in England; and when their branches are in full leaf, must be extremely picturesque. Even in the winter time, these groups of well-grown trees

. . . have a very quaint appearance, seeming to bring about a kind of compromise between town and country.[1]

However, Yale's alumni, like Harvard's, showed no affection for the simple red brick Georgian buildings that were beginning to be associated with the less-than-noble colonial past. Moreover, red brick had become the preferred material for mill construction in New England, so its associations, as at Harvard, were with business-like utility, an idea not then held in the high regard it today enjoys in some academic quarters. In his autobiography, Andrew Dickson White, an 1853 graduate of Yale who went on to become the first president of Cornell, recalled that during his

life at Yale . . . [he] had been painfully impressed by the lack of any development of that which might be called the commemorative or poetical element. In the long row of barracks at Yale one longed for some bit of beauty, and hungered and thirsted for something which connected the present with the past; but . . . there was little more

TOP
College Row, 1807.

ABOVE
Connecticut Hall, 1753.

LEFT
New Haven's nine-square plan, 1641.

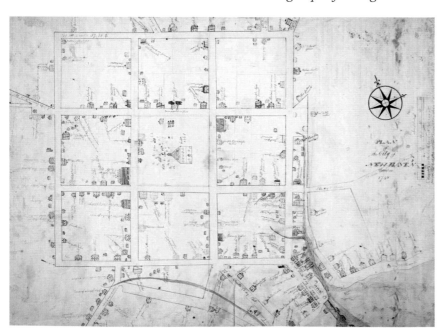

to feed the sense of beauty or to meet one's craving for commemoration of the past than in a cotton-factory.[2]

Yale turned to Gothic styling in 1846 with Henry Austin's library, evocative of an English cathedral and complimented as the first college building to make any "pretensions to architectural beauty."[3] Significantly, Yale's first building not constructed facing the city, the library was set well behind the brick row and entered from the garden-like campus of the block's interior. Six years later, Alexander Jackson Davis's Gothic-style Alumni Hall (1853), conveying a more militaristic aspect—suggesting castles rather than churches—implied that Yale's honeymoon with New Haven had not led to a particularly happy marriage. Students had rioted regularly during the eighteenth century and New Havenites resented being taxed for the repairs. By the 1850s town-gown relations had gotten pretty out of hand, with one scuffle in 1854 resulting in a town mob leader being stabbed to death, and in 1856 a fireman was shot and killed by a student. While it is not clear who was more at fault—the town or the gown—by the end of the Civil War, as New Haven prospered, it was clear that Yale needed a greater barrier than a wood fence to maintain its collegiate tone in the bustling city. Consequently, College Row gave way to a continuous

palisade of battlemented Gothic dormitories that presented a solid wall to the New Haven Green and were entered from the interior of what was becoming less a campus in the sense of "field" and more a quadrangle such as was to be seen at the universities of Oxford and Cambridge in England. By 1900 only one vestige was left of the "Old Brick Row": Connecticut Hall, now an object of veneration, safely marooned behind the palisade.

Even though Yale had embraced the Gothic in the 1840s and generally stayed with it through the 1890s, the university entered the new century by celebrating the bicentennial of its founding with a bold plan and group of buildings to be realized on a significant portion of a second of New Haven's original nine squares, now referred to as the New Campus. The sponsors of the university's Bicentennial Buildings (Carrère & Hastings, 1901–2) rejected romanticized Collegiate Gothic in favor of a grandiose modern classicism: however, style aside, the Bicentennial Buildings, like those on what by then was coming to be known as the Old Campus, were conceived as the first components of a future quadrangle that would not be realized until the 1930s, when a library, dormitories, and classroom buildings would complete the other two of its four walls.

The monumental classicism of the Bicentennial Buildings proved aberrant, but the idea of strategic quadrangular insertions into the city's street grid did not. Located across the street from the Old

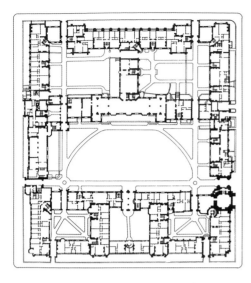

ABOVE
*Harkness Memorial
Quadrangle plan, James
Gamble Rogers, 1921.*

RIGHT
*Harkness Memorial
Quadrangle, James
Gamble Rogers, 1921.*

BELOW
*Davenport College, James
Gamble Rogers, 1932.*

Campus, James Gamble Rogers's Harkness Memorial Quadrangle (1917) was deliberately conceived in emulation of those at Oxford and Cambridge. At the time Rogers was asked to design the Harkness Quadrangle he had never visited either Oxford or Cambridge and though he quickly did so he also relied extensively on photographs to provide him with the all-important details. With the Memorial Quadrangle Rogers achieved a complex balance between academic seclusion and the gritty realities of an industrialized city that would be Yale's development template for a generation or more. For its extensive decorative embellishments he mined both the history of Yale and its relationship to the city of New Haven.

The Harkness Quadrangle's success as an urbanistically embedded collegiate retreat depended on Rogers's masterly layout as much as on the luxurious historicizing and iconographic detail. Capitalizing on the classical planning that was a legacy of six years of study at the École des Beaux-Arts, Rogers aerated the 335-by-396-foot quadrangle with six courtyards, providing a small scale and variety that the Old Campus quadrangle lacked. At once a secret garden and a city within a city, the quadrangle was separated from the surrounding streets by lushly planted moats, interrupted by entryways leading to the inner courtyards from which the various student suites, dining halls, and libraries were accessible.

Realizing that the college had grown into a major university, threatening the intimacies of undergraduate life, in 1926 Edward S. Harkness extended his family's generosity by proposing a plan for a residential college system based on the Memorial Quadrangle. At that time, boarding off campus was the norm

for most Yale undergraduates. Harkness felt that "average men" were missing out on much of the fraternal experience college life should include. Together with Yale's president James Rowland Angell, Harkness and Rogers traveled to England to study the residential life of colleges at Oxford and Cambridge. There they found individual scholastic environments, with each college containing a master's house, living suites, dining halls, and study commons for a relatively small, cohesive group of students—an organic communal experience derived from monastic models. But Yale's trustees were reluctant to further indulge Harkness's dream of a medieval Oxbridge in Connecticut. An angered Harkness took his money to rival Harvard, donating, in December 1928, eleven million dollars to a university where neither he nor any of his family had studied. Harvard undertook a residential plan such as Harkness had intended to sponsor at Yale and built the so-called River Houses. Yale, realizing the foolishness of its decision, applied to Harkness to fund its own residential college program, which seemed all the more desirable after the humiliation of losing the funds to Harvard. Remarkably, Harkness still

ABOVE LEFT
*Sterling Law Library,
James Gamble Rogers, 1931.*

ABOVE RIGHT
*Sterling Divinity School,
Delano & Aldrich, 1932.*

had enough money left over—fifteen million dollars—to pay for eight new quadrangular colleges at Yale, begun in 1930. The budget was far less lavish than that of the Memorial Quadrangle, but Yale made do.

Under Rogers's direction, Yale's expansion of the 1930s enabled it to reinvent its own history in steel, brick, and stone. As Rogers designed them, the Yale colleges made up an architectural pedigree for the university, taking students on a journey through centuries of architectural history but realized in little more than a decade. In the Memorial Quadrangle Rogers had used architecture to provide Yale with a kind of WASP version of *Roots,* with each important event in Yale's history, and each important teacher and graduate, memorialized in stone. With the eight new colleges, the historical intention was similar but the means quite different. True, some of the new colleges extended the Oxbridge metaphor, but others, perhaps reflecting the revival of interest in colonial Georgian architecture inspired by the reconstruction of Colonial Williamsburg, led Rogers to push Yale's architectural story toward a recapitulation of its Georgian-era opening chapters.

Whether Georgian or Gothic, Yale's colleges brilliantly accommodated the pastoral ideal to the circumstances of urban life. Hemmed in by the city, the quadrangular colleges turned Yale inward, preserving its identity as a place apart, so that by the end of the 1930s Yale, now grown to the scale of Columbia and Harvard, was a big place made up of many small places, not a university city but a university in a city.

Just as Harvard expanded to Holmes Field in order to provide space for its growing programs, so Yale moved north beyond its real estate in the original nine-square plan of New Haven, threading its way along existing streets, building where it could but establishing in the 1920s two new mini-campuses, such as Harvard Business School, but in this case housing a divinity school (Delano & Aldrich, 1932) that evoked Jefferson's UVA and a science campus with Gothic buildings arrayed on the perimeter so as to reinforce the connection between the sciences and the humanities that constituted the university's pedagogical bedrock.

After World War II, returning to the stylistic eclecticism that they had pursued in the nineteenth century, many older universities peppered their campuses with a sampling of highly individualistic, up-to-the-minute architecture. This approach took hold most brilliantly at Yale, where, under Eero Saarinen's leadership as master planner, a series of buildings was commissioned that transformed the

TOP
Beinecke Library, Skidmore Owings & Merrill, 1963.

ABOVE
Ingalls Hockey Rink, Eero Saarinen, 1958.

BELOW
Yale University Art Gallery, Louis I. Kahn, 1953.

derived from the work of Frank Lloyd Wright and Le Corbusier to push modernism toward contextualism, echoing in mass Yale's many-towered Gothic skyline. Furthering this sense of contextualism, Saarinen's design for two new residential colleges, Morse and Stiles (1962) proved most significant from the point of view of campus urbanism. Before Saarinen's, the last college to be built on campus was Silliman College in 1940, cobbled together from a stylistically diverse collection of earlier buildings already on the site and new ones in the Georgian style. In response to an unattractive site squeezed between Gothic-style buildings from the 1930s and perhaps in deference to the value of the traditional colleges on campus he had enjoyed as a student at Yale, Saarinen made a decisive break with the modernist orthodoxies of his work for corporations like General Motors and IBM, designing two cloistered groupings of low buildings punctuated by towers separated by a twisting and turning pedestrian street such as one might find in an Italian hill town. Though he "conceived of the colleges as Citadels of Masonry,"[4] there was not the money—or perhaps the will—to use brick and stone as Rogers had, so Saarinen experimented until he devised "masonry walls made without masons"[5] by spraying concrete around rough boulders casually laid up.

campus into something of an outdoor museum of modernism, but one that was strictly framed by traditional architecture. The first of the modernist buildings at Yale, Louis Kahn's Art Gallery (1953), wrapped blank brick and glass walls around a loft-like structure spanned by a structurally innovative tetrahedral ceiling. The Art Gallery was Kahn's first masterpiece, but for many years the university's confidence in the building and its architect wavered. However, Kahn's last building, the Yale Center for British Art (1977), occupies a site across the street from the Art Gallery and was more immediately embraced. Saarinen's Ingalls Hockey Rink (1958) is a structural tour-de-force that batters at the gates of Yale's Science Hill, while Gordon Bunshaft's Beinecke Library (1963) more sympathetically takes its place in an enlarged frame bounded by Rogers's Gothic Law School (1931) and the Carrère & Hastings Bicentennial Buildings. Paul Rudolph's Art & Architecture Building (1963) went even further, with tropes

Saarinen's chief complaint about the older colleges at Yale was that they closed themselves off from the city. He wanted the citizens of New Haven to walk right through his colleges. After his death, his widow fought to keep the university from building gates across the entrances. Yale compromised, promising to keep the gates open during the day. Now they are always locked, a return to the realistic appraisal of the gulf between the town and the campus that had spurred Rogers to include moats in his original designs for Yale forty years before, that had led President Porter to surround the Old Campus with a continuous wall of buildings, and had driven Jefferson deep into the countryside to lay out the University of Virginia at the dawn of the republic.

As this is being written, we are deep into the design of two new residential colleges for Yale, to be located on Prospect Street, the principal campus spine connecting the Old and New campuses with Science Hill and the Divinity School. Before undertaking this challenge, as a warm-up, so to speak, we designed Maurice R. Greenberg Conference Center (2009), a small building appended to Betts House, a Victorian-era mansion (Henry Austin and David R. Brown, 1868) restored in 2002 to serve as headquarters for Yale's Global Fellows program. Comprising seminar and breakout rooms, an 88-seat auditorium provisioned for simultaneous language translation, and a 98-seat dining

hall, Greenberg Hall was designed to say "Yale" by conveying the Gothic character of the central campus to university visitors who may not have the chance to experience it directly.

Our two new colleges, housing 425 students each, will occupy a 6.2-acre site bisected by a pedestrian walk. Conceived as fraternal twins, similar in size but each enjoying its own identity, they will be in Gothic style, using brick and stone with each college containing variously scaled courtyards in the manner of Rogers's Harkness Memorial Quadrangle. Echoing Rogers's environmentally responsive massing, the heights of the buildings will rise from south to north to allow for maximum sunlight in the courts. The new colleges will take their place on Yale's skyline with a variety of dramatically modeled towers.

1. Charles Dickens, *American Notes,* quoted in Paul Venable Turner, *Campus: An American Planning Tradition* (New York: The Architectural History Foundation; Cambridge, Mass. and London: The MIT Press, 1984), 101.
2. Andrew Dickson White, *Autobiography* I: 407, quoted in Albert Bush-Brown, *Image of a University: A Study of Architecture as an Expression of Education at Colleges and Universities in the United States between 1800 and 1900* (Princeton, N.J.: Princeton University Press 1958), 186–87.
3. Lyman Hotchkiss Bagg, *Four Years at Yale* (New Haven, Conn: Chatfield, 1871), quoted in Reuben A. Holden, *Yale: A Pictorial History* (New Haven, Conn.: Yale University Press, 1976), unpaginated.
4. Eero Saarinen, *Eero Saarinen on His Work*. ed. Aline B. Saarinen, rev. ed. (New Haven, Conn.: Yale University Press, 1968), 88.
5. Ibid.

ABOVE LEFT
Art and Architecture Building (now Rudolph Hall), Paul Rudolph, 1963.

ABOVE RIGHT
Morse and Stiles Colleges, Eero Saarinen, 1962.

YALE UNIVERSITY
CAMPUS PLAN

Entry porch looking to Betts House and the tower of the Divinity School.

OVERLEAF
West facade.

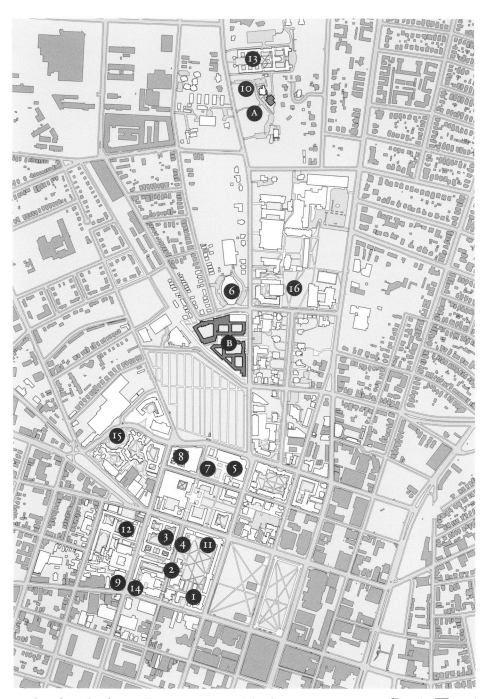

A. Greenberg Conference Center
B. New Residential Colleges
1. Connecticut Hall
2. Yale College Library (now Dwight Hall)
3. Harkness Memorial Quad
4. Harkness Tower
5. Bicentennial Buildings
6. Ingalls Hockey Rink
7. Beinecke Library
8. Law School
9. Art and Architecture Building (now Rudolph Hall)
10. Betts House
11. Farnam Hall
12. Davenport College
13. Sterling Divinity School
14. Art Gallery
15. Morse and Stiles Colleges
16. Science Hill

0   300   600 FT

GREENBERG
CONFERENCE CENTER

2006–2009

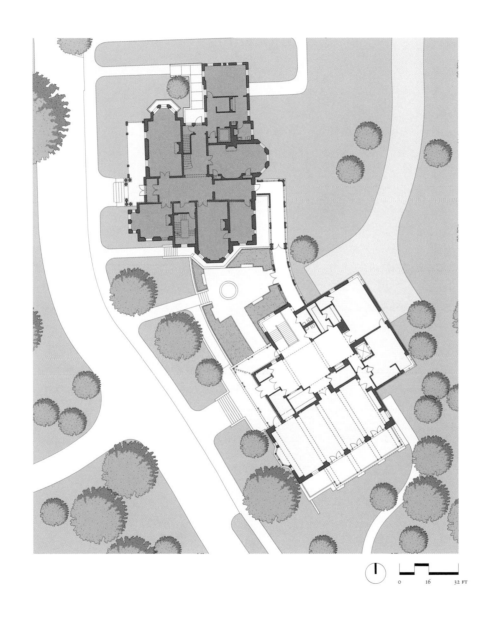

LEFT
Connector to Betts House.

RIGHT TOP
Lobby.
Lower lobby.

RIGHT BOTTOM
Auditorium.
Conference room.

OVERLEAF
Dining room.

RESIDENTIAL COLLEGES

2008–

SACHEM STREET

PROSPECT WALK

PROSPECT STREET

FARMINGTON CANAL TRAIL

0   50   100 FT

LEFT TOP
*View looking west across
Prospect Street.
Small courtyard, south
college.*

LEFT BOTTOM
*Main courtyard, north
college.
View looking north
along Prospect Street.*

RIGHT
*Small courtyard, north
college.*

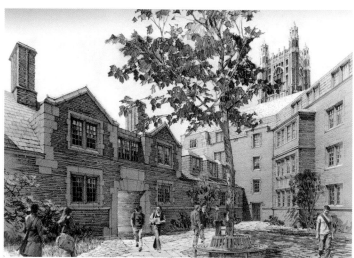

UNIVERSITY OF PENNSYLVANIA

PHILADELPHIA, PENNSYLVANIA. In 1872 the University of Pennsylvania moved to its third campus, occupying sprawling acreage between a gritty industrial area along the Schuylkill River and the fashionable suburb of West Philadelphia. Although its previous campus in the center of Philadelphia had been conceived with some sense of ensemble, the West Philadelphia campus evolved as a collection of independently massed, frequently aggressively styled buildings set with no particular relationship one to the other, a situation that was somewhat redressed in the first two decades of the twentieth century with the construction of Cope & Stewardson and Frank Miles Day's quadrangular ensemble of Gothic-style undergraduate residence halls.

In the 1950s, after the construction hiatus caused by the Great Depression and World War II, and despite a number of efforts to impose a rigorous planning discipline, Penn returned to its typical practice of individualistic buildings, this time not reflecting historicizing eclecticism but instead zeitgeist-driven modernism.

In the late 1980s, building upon previous efforts by landscape architects George Patton and Peter Shepheard to develop an overriding order to Penn's campus, Laurie Olin, also a landscape architect, recognized the university's almost genetic resistance to large-scale planning and concentrated instead on the development of individual focal outdoor spaces. Strengthening Woodland Walk, formerly a diagonal arterial street that cut through the campus, Olin created a prominent gateway site at the intersection of Thirty-fourth and Walnut Streets, where it was subsequently decided to locate our McNeil Center for Early American Studies (2005).

The McNeil Center seeks to satisfy its scholarly purpose with a design mediating between the university's art historically driven mandate that each new building reflect the time of its construction and the donor's preference for an architecture reflecting the early years of the American Republic to which the center is dedicated. To further complicate this challenge, the McNeil Center is a small building in a very big setting. Moreover, the neighboring buildings designs, are mostly irregularly massed

Tudorbethan, including Oswald Shelly's Phi Delta Theta Fraternity (1900) and Thomas Churchman and Walter H. Thomas's Zeta Psi Fraternity (1909) on two of the other corners. Only Cope & Stewardson's Law School (old style figs.) engages with Georgian Philadelphia, albeit by way of Wrenian Baroque. Eero Saarinen's Hill College House (1958) is also nearby.

To this end, the McNeil Center is decidedly not stylistically contextual. Its massing and sparingly detailed flattened red brick facades reflect on the one hand late-eighteenth- and early-nineteenth-century Philadelphia precedents, in particular William Russell Birch's Library and Surgeons Hall (1799), his proposed President's House, and Benjamin Henry Latrobe's Medical School (1810), and on the other, Louis I. Kahn's way of handling brick in various of his buildings. In so doing the McNeil Center connects both with Philadelphia's early architectural history and with the work of its most distinguished architectural alumnus, whose work resonates with the architecture of his university and his city.

ABOVE
Library and Surgeons Hall, William Russell Birch, 1799.

LEFT
Zeta Psi Fraternity, Thomas Churchman and William H. Thomas, 1909.

BELOW
Hill College House, Eero Saarinen, 1958.

UNIVERSITY OF PENNSYLVANIA
CAMPUS PLAN

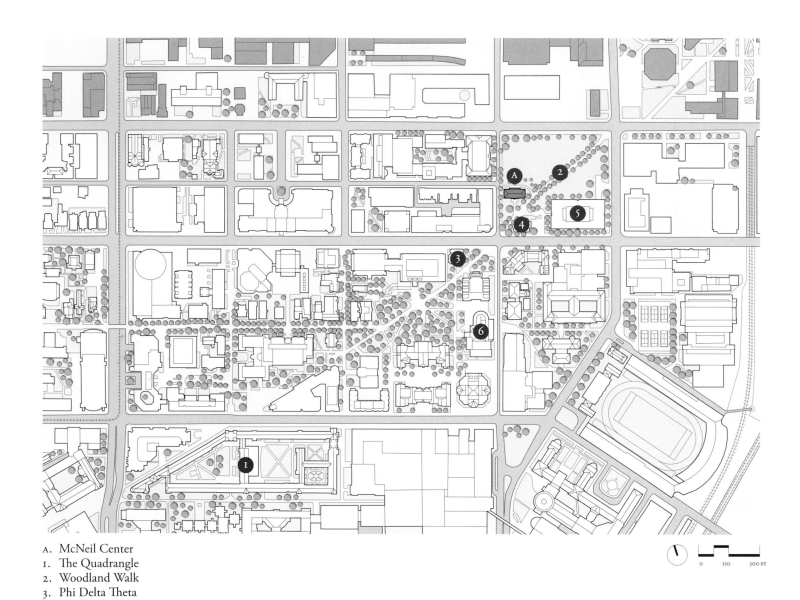

A. McNeil Center
1. The Quadrangle
2. Woodland Walk
3. Phi Delta Theta
4. Zeta Psi Fraternity
5. Hill College House
6. University Library (now
   Fisher Fine Arts Library)

0   150   300 FT

McNeil Center for Early American Studies

2003–2005

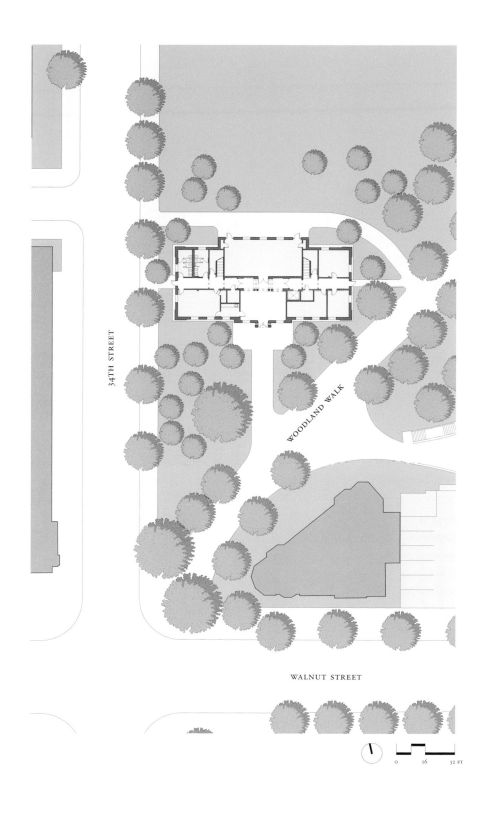

34TH STREET

WOODLAND WALK

WALNUT STREET

0   16   32 FT

LEFT
Reception room.

RIGHT TOP
Library.

RIGHT BOTTOM
Lecture room.

BROWN
UNIVERSITY

PROVIDENCE, RHODE ISLAND. Brown was founded in 1764 by a group of Baptists acting in response to the establishment of Harvard and Yale by other religious denominations. Its first building, University Hall (1770), which Montgomery Schuyler described as "the perfectly unpretentious, perfectly practical, and as nearly as possible inexpressive work of the Colonial bricklayer,"[1] housed all of the college functions until a near twin, Hope College, was built as a dormitory in 1822, soon to be followed by the imposing Greek revival Manning Hall (1834). By 1900 serviceable buildings had been interspersed among the houses and churches of College Hill, many facing College Green, the main campus open space.

Center, the Coleman Aquatics Center, and the Zucconi Varsity Strength and Conditioning Center, all in a single building, now under construction toward completion in 2012, bounding the south side of what is to be the landscaped Ittleson Quadrangle. Facing Hope Street, the Fitness Center acknowledges Brown's historic tradition of simple brick buildings, and in particular the much-missed Marvel Gymnasium (1927), the cupola of which, saved when the building was demolished in 2002, will cap the roof of the new building.

As Brown grew to university status in the early twentieth century, low-key red brick Georgian quadrangles were realized on various sites, further embedding the college into its architecturally distinguished neighborhood.

After World War II, the university underwent a major expansion, constructing many brutalist buildings. Among these, the Erickson Athletic Complex, combining playing fields and various indoor sports venues, occupied a large parcel of land that had been the grounds of the former Dexter asylum, a "poor farm." Regrettably, none of the buildings comprising the Erickson Complex was designed to form a coherent group, so that the whole has an ad-hoc feel, with little concern given to the architecture and urbanism of the surrounding neighborhood or to pedestrian circulation between the central campus and the playing fields.

A 2006 campus plan by Kliment & Halsband led to our design of the Fitness and Aquatics Center, incorporating the Nelson Fitness

1. Montgomery Schuyler, "Architecture of American Campuses VII—Brown, Bowdoin, Trinity, and Wesleyan," *Architectural Record* 29 (February 1911): 148.

BROWN UNIVERSITY
CAMPUS PLAN

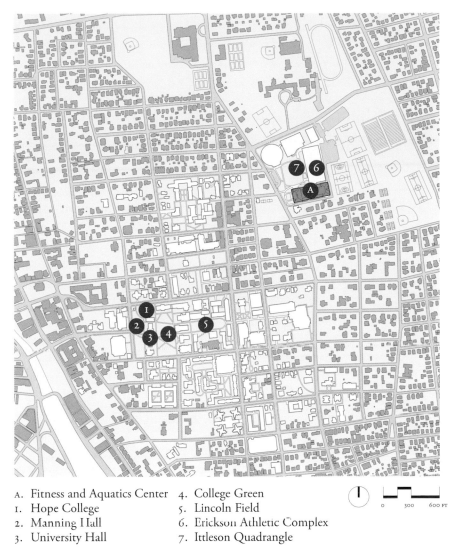

A. Fitness and Aquatics Center
1. Hope College
2. Manning Hall
3. University Hall

4. College Green
5. Lincoln Field
6. Erickson Athletic Complex
7. Ittleson Quadrangle

0   300   600 FT

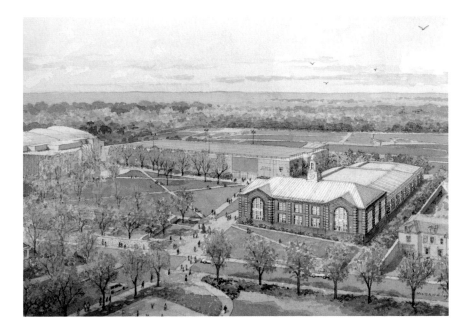

UNIVERSITY OF MICHIGAN

ANN ARBOR, MICHIGAN. The University of Michigan was founded in 1817 in Detroit as the Catholepistemiad, or University of Michigania, about twenty years before the Michigan Territory officially became a state. In 1837 it was relocated to Ann Arbor, originally occupying forty acres of land, but growing in size so that its more than 500 buildings now sprawl across over 1400 acres on two campuses, separated by the Huron River. The forty-acre square that is the Central Campus is in many ways similar to Harvard's Yard or Yale's Old Campus. But unlike the Yard and Old Campus, the Central Campus is at once the heart of the university and of the town.

Not coincidentally, given his work in New Haven, Alexander Jackson Davis, commissioned to design the first building for the newly established Ann Arbor campus, proposed an elaborately detailed Gothic U-shaped quadrangle that proved too expensive. However, Davis may have been responsible for the plan of buildings that were built in the 1830s and 1840s in emulation of John Trumbull's Brick Row at Yale and for the decision to fill out the remainder of the forty-acre property with a Botanical Garden.

ABOVE
Hill Auditorium, Albert Kahn, 1913.

BELOW
Law School, York & Sawyer, 1933.

By the early 1900s, the Central Campus was no longer able to house the many departments of what was well on its way to becoming a major university, and expansion northeast into the town led to the establishment of a new academic complex facing a new quarter-mile-long Campus Mall, lined by buildings designed by Michigan's leading architect, Albert Kahn, in a Prairie-Style version of classicism. The university also expanded to the south of the Central Campus, where the Law School (1933), designed by York & Sawyer, as if to counteract Kahn's regional classicism, reflected the Collegiate Gothic of Yale. University buildings were also realized on various scattered sites, one

of which across State Street from the Central Campus was the much admired and beloved Michigan Union (1919) by Allen B. and Irving K. Pond, an inventive combination of Collegiate Gothic massing and Arts and Crafts detail, built as the student center for men. Its complement for women, the Michigan League (1929), also designed by Pond and Pond, is also widely admired, as is Emil Lorch's College of Architecture (1928, now Lorch Hall), a brick structure with sloping slate roofs. All three, but especially the Union, inspired our work at Weill Hall (2006) and at the North Quad (2010).

Conceived as a welcoming landmark, Joan and Sanford Weill Hall, home to the Gerald R. Ford School of Public Policy, is the first University of Michigan academic building encountered on approaching the campus from the south, where a tower culminates the building's composition of variegated decorative red brickwork highlighted by bright stone. Weill Hall takes advantage of the change in grade across the site to allow for what are effectively two ground floors along the path of travel through the building, with a lower gateway entrance at the base of the tower and a more intimate entry one level above on a courtyard facing the law school's campus to the north. A generously proportioned, naturally lit stair provides the building with a dramatic vertical spine connecting all levels, and together with wide corridors and alcoves of various shapes

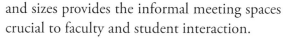

and sizes provides the informal meeting spaces crucial to faculty and student interaction.

The North Quad Residential and Academic Complex represents a new university initiative to combine undergraduate living, learning, and academic support in one building. Located on a full block anchoring the northwest corner of the main campus, with massing and forms based on the blend of Collegiate Gothic and Arts and Crafts seen at the Michigan Union, the Michigan League, and Lorch Hall, North Quad carries forward the strategy we followed in designing Weill Hall, realizing the surfaces of a large building as a rich tapestry of deep red brick, stone, and slate. Interconnected courtyards aerate the complex, while welcoming plazas at the northwest and southeast corners of the block open the quad to its surroundings. The composition rises in a counterclockwise spiral to a bold tower that terminates the axis of South Thayer Street, joining other nearby towers that enliven the Central Campus skyline.

TOP LEFT
Michigan Union, Pond and Pond, 1919.

TOP RIGHT
College of Architecture (now Lorch Hall), Emil Lorch, 1928.

ABOVE
Michigan League, Pond and Pond, 1929.

RIGHT
View looking northeast.

OVERLEAF
*View looking south along
South State Street past
the Law School (York &
Sawyer, 1929–33).*

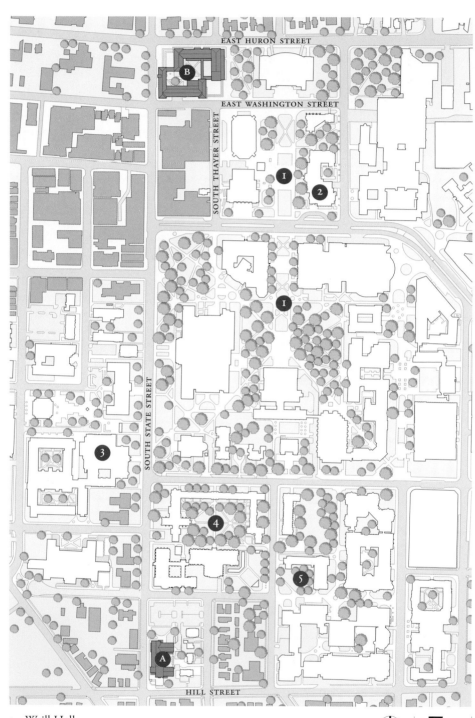

A. Weill Hall
B. North Quad
1. Campus Mall
2. Michigan League
3. Michigan Union
4. Law School
5. Lorch Hall

0   140   280 FT

WEILL HALL

GERALD R. FORD SCHOOL OF PUBLIC POLICY

2002–2006

North entry.

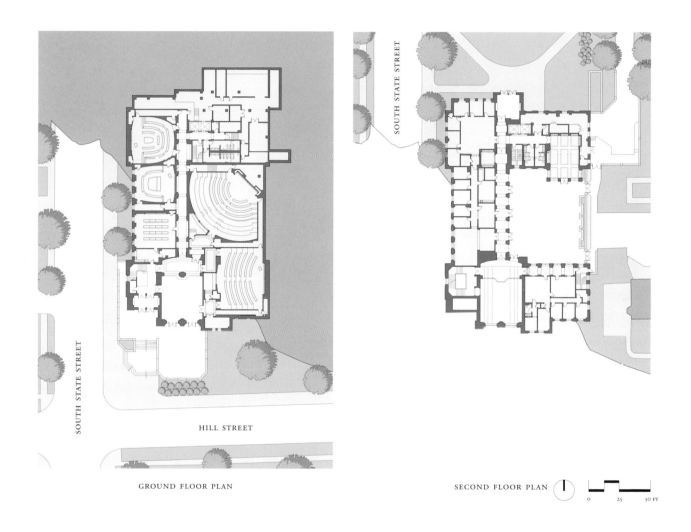

SOUTH STATE STREET

HILL STREET

GROUND FLOOR PLAN

SECOND FLOOR PLAN

0   25   50 FT

LEFT TOP
Main stair.

LEFT BOTTOM
*Circulation desk at Towsley
Reading Room.*

RIGHT TOP
Great Hall.

RIGHT BOTTOM
Annenberg Auditorium.

NORTH QUAD
RESIDENTIAL AND
ACADEMIC COMPLEX

2006–2010

PREVIOUS PAGES
*View looking southeast
from East Huron and
South State Streets*

LEFT
*View looking north from
South Thayer Street.*

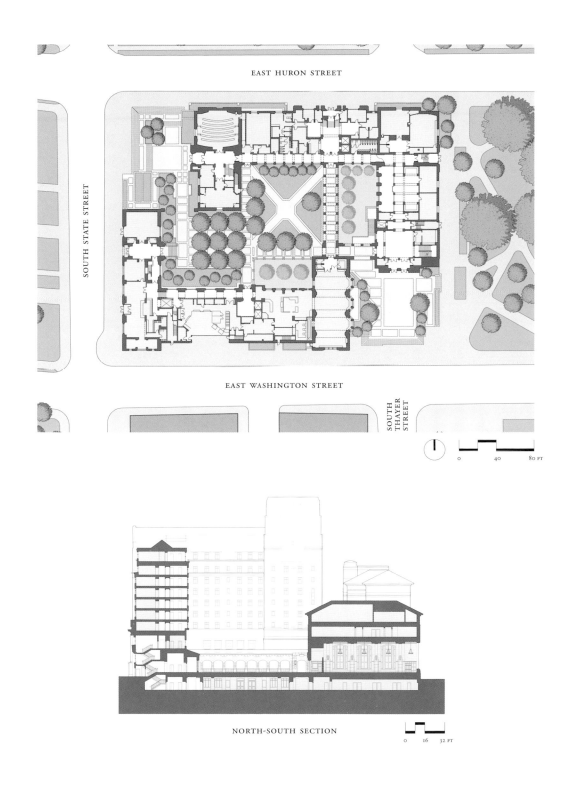

EAST HURON STREET

SOUTH STATE STREET

EAST WASHINGTON STREET

SOUTH THAYER STREET

0   40   80 FT

NORTH-SOUTH SECTION

0   16   32 FT

LEFT
*Entry to residential
building at northwest
plaza.*

RIGHT
*Covered entry to courtyard
at southeast plaza.*

BROOKLYN LAW SCHOOL

BROOKLYN, NEW YORK. Brooklyn Law School, founded in 1901 by William Payson Richardson and Norman P. Heffley, was initially housed in the basement of Heffley's business school. By 1929 it had become sufficiently well established to occupy an eight-story limestone and brick Romanesque-inspired facility designed by Mayers, Murray & Phillip, successors to Bertram Grosvenor Goodhue.

BROOKLYN
LAW SCHOOL
TOWER

1990–1994

FEIL HALL

2000–2005

PREVIOUS PAGES
State Street entrance.

LEFT
*View from State Street and
Boerum Place.*

OVERLEAF
Forchelli Conference Room.

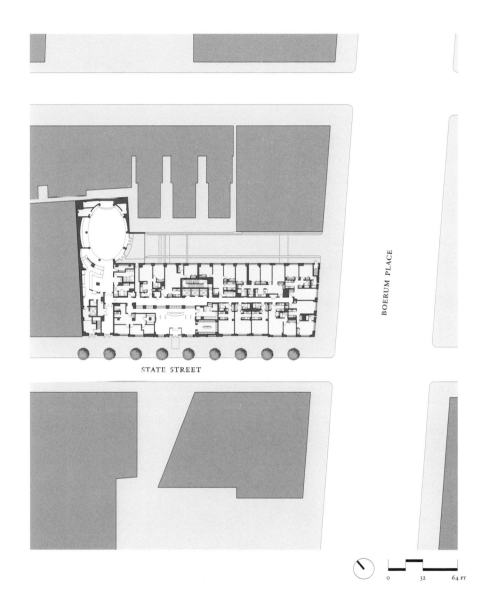

STATE STREET

BOERUM PLACE

0   32   64 FT

SALVE REGINA UNIVERSITY

NEWPORT, RHODE ISLAND. Chartered in 1934, Salve Regina first opened its doors in 1947 when the opportunity arose for it to take over one of the great "cottages" of Newport's Gilded Age, the Goelet family's Ochre Court (Richard Morris Hunt, 1891). Since then Salve has embedded itself in Newport's summer colony, occupying Wakehurst (Charles Eamer Kempe, 1888) and other houses, including H. H. Richardson's Watts Sherman House (1876), as well as Peabody & Stearns's Vinland, including the main house for Catherine Lorillard Wolfe (1882) and the Hennery (1885).

The Rodgers Recreation Center (2000) was designed in response to concerns that a contemplated indoor athletic facility would overwhelm its site, an open field between Ochre Court and a residential neighborhood. Accommodating a significant portion of the facility's program below ground, we designed the above-ground portion in the manner of the late-nineteenth-century shingle style buildings that abound in the area.

Nestled among the buildings and established landscape of the Vinland estate (Peabody & Stearns, 1882), and lit by a set of stained glass windows designed by John LaFarge in the 1890s, Our Lady of Mercy Chapel (2010) combines local stone with cedar shingles. The chapel is sited to make explicit the relationship between Ochre Court and Vinland, helping to bind them into a cohesive academic group.

Salve has also built various new buildings, but these have not necessarily reflected their rich architectural setting.

SALVE REGINA UNIVERSITY
CAMPUS PLAN

A. Rodgers Recreation Center
B. Our Lady of Mercy Chapel
1. Ochre Court
2. Wakehurst
3. Hennery
4. Vinland
5. McKillop Library

RODGERS
RECREATION CENTER

1997–2000

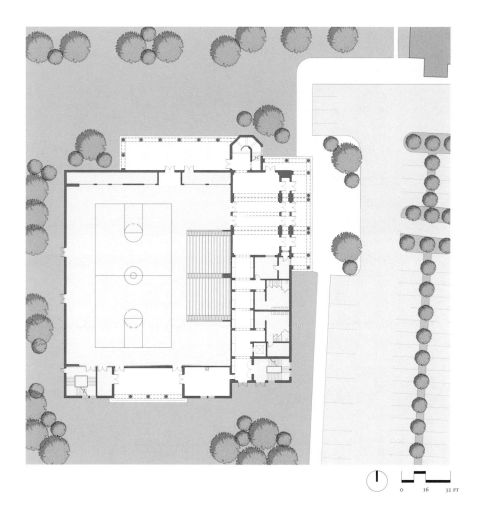

LEFT TOP
South facade.

LEFT BOTTOM
View looking northwest.

RIGHT
East entrance.

LEFT
Stair.

RIGHT TOP
Trophy hall.

RIGHT BOTTOM
Upper-floor gallery looking to gymnasium.

OVERLEAF
Aerial view looking west.

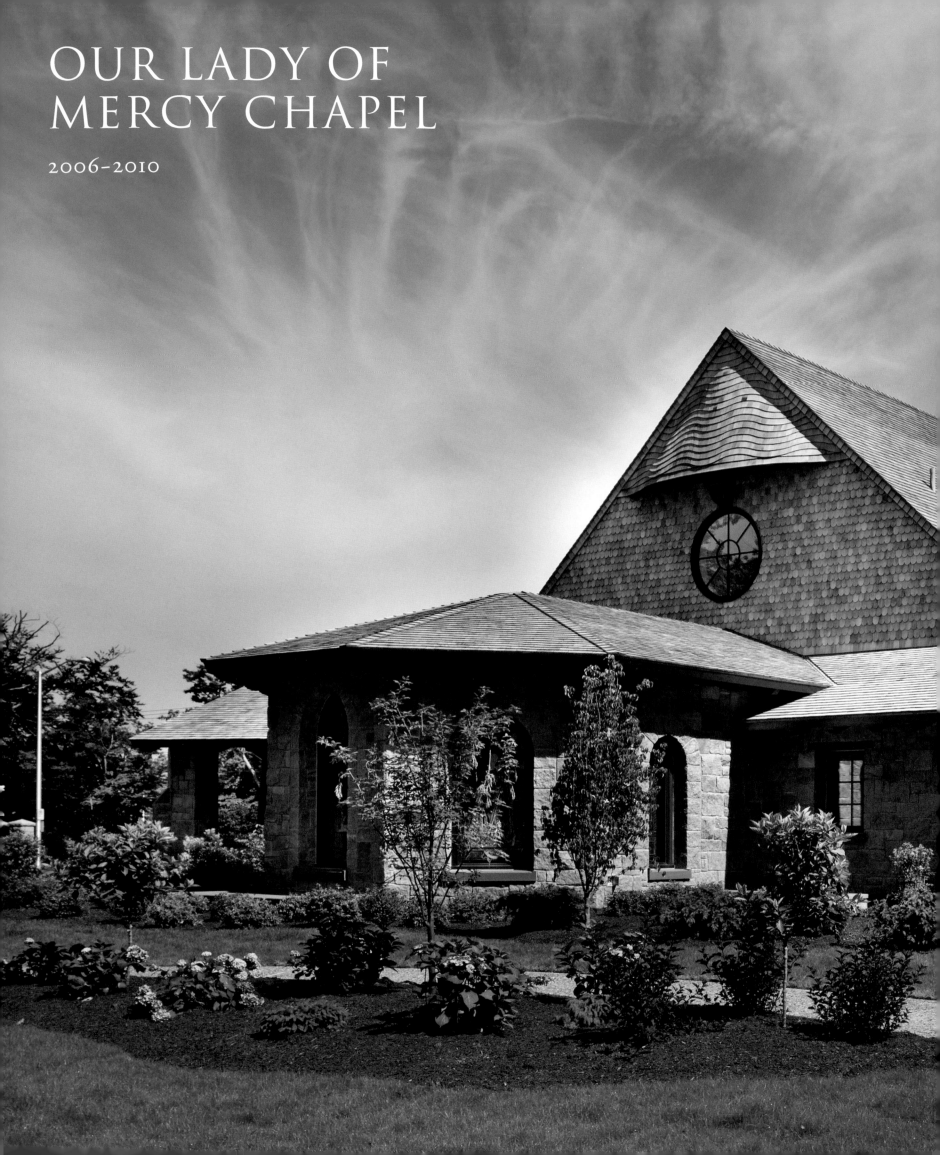

OUR LADY OF MERCY CHAPEL

2006–2010

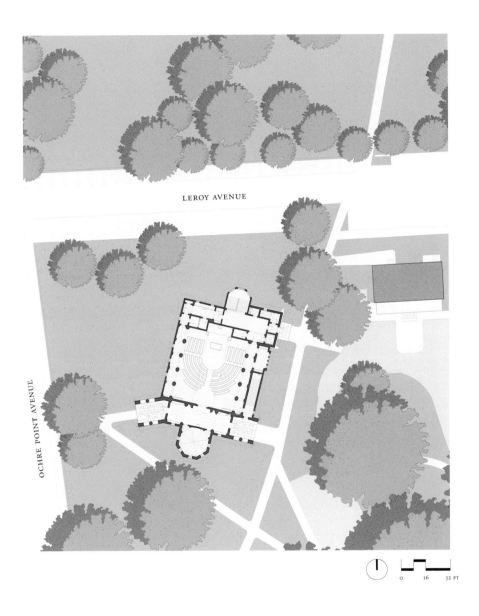

LEROY AVENUE

OCHRE POINT AVENUE

0   16   32 FT

UNIVERSITY OF CALIFORNIA LOS ANGELES

LOS ANGELES, CALIFORNIA. UCLA, with roots stretching back to its founding in 1881 as the Los Angeles State Normal School, joined the University of California system in 1919 as the university's Southern Branch. Soon afterward the institution moved to a campus in the planned neighborhood of Westwood, with limestone-trimmed tawny brick, red-tile-roofed Lombardy Romanesque-inspired buildings by its planner, George W. Kelham, and by the firm Allison & Allison.

DARTMOUTH COLLEGE

HANOVER, NEW HAMPSHIRE. Founded in 1769, Dartmouth College constitutes something of an anomaly among embedded campuses. The college was not established in an existing town as Harvard and Yale were, but rather along with the town of Hanover, New Hampshire. Conceived as one, college and town were each intended to support the other, sharing a central green—significantly named after the college.

Soon after its founding, Dartmouth realized three buildings facing the green: four-square Georgian boxes arranged in an A-B-A manner, not unlike Yale's Brick Row. In the early twentieth century, Charles Rich met the needs of the growing college with additional buildings facing the green, mixing Beaux-Arts mass with Georgian character. Rich's buildings enabled the college to meet modern programmatic requirements, but threatened to overwhelm the scale of the town.

MOORE PSYCHOLOGY BUILDING

1992–1999

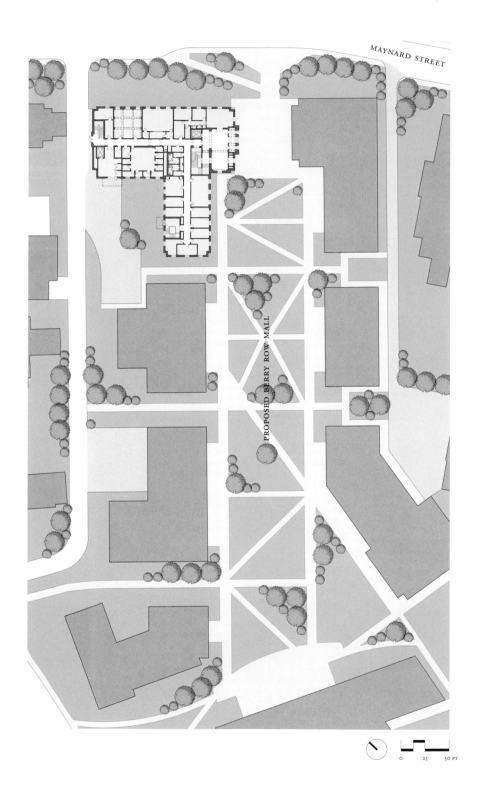

MAYNARD STREET

PROPOSED BERRY ROW MALL

0   25   50 FT

MIAMI
UNIVERSITY

OXFORD, OHIO. Miami University, the ultimate embedded campus where town and college are virtually one and the same, was established in 1809 as a consequence of Ohio's admission to statehood six years earlier, with the requirement that a township be set aside for an academy, but it was not until 1824 that the university got started in earnest. The university's early history was rocky—it was closed between 1873 and 1885—but by the early 1900s, with support from the State of Ohio, Miami began to prosper.

FARMER SCHOOL
OF BUSINESS

2004–2009

PREVIOUS PAGES
South courtyard.

LEFT
North facade.

OVERLEAF
Forsythe Commons.

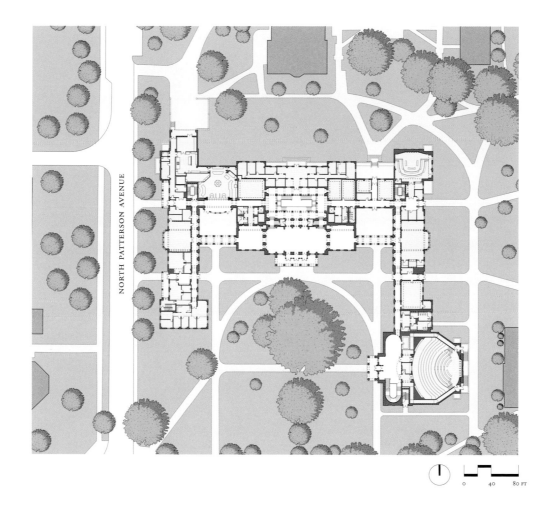

NORTH PATTERSON AVENUE

0   40   80 FT

ST. PAUL'S SCHOOL

CONCORD, NEW HAMPSHIRE. Private academies, many of them restricted to boarding students, can be traced back to the earliest days of the republic, predating the rise of public school education in the 1840s. Phillips Academy, the country's oldest incorporated boarding school, was established in 1778 in a single building housing sixty boys on 141 acres of land in Andover, Massachusetts. Three years later it was followed by Phillips Academy in Exeter, New Hampshire. By the end of the nineteenth century, the number of boarding schools increased, at first slowly, and then exponentially in the 1890s.

ST. PAUL'S SCHOOL
CAMPUS PLAN

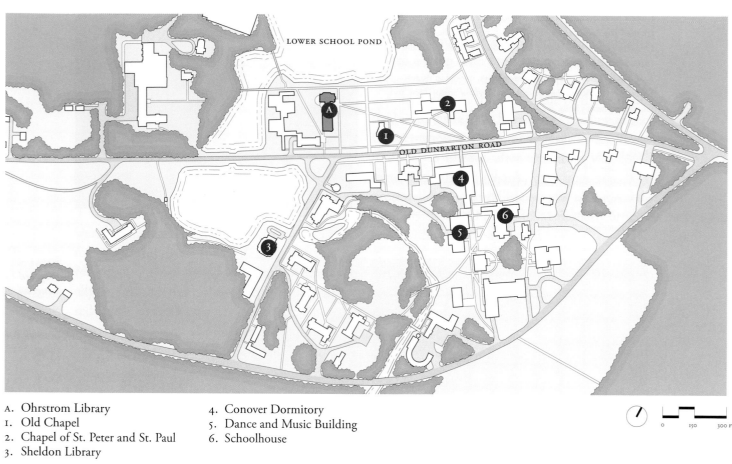

LOWER SCHOOL POND

OLD DUNBARTON ROAD

A. Ohrstrom Library
1. Old Chapel
2. Chapel of St. Peter and St. Paul
3. Sheldon Library

4. Conover Dormitory
5. Dance and Music Building
6. Schoolhouse

0   150   300 FT

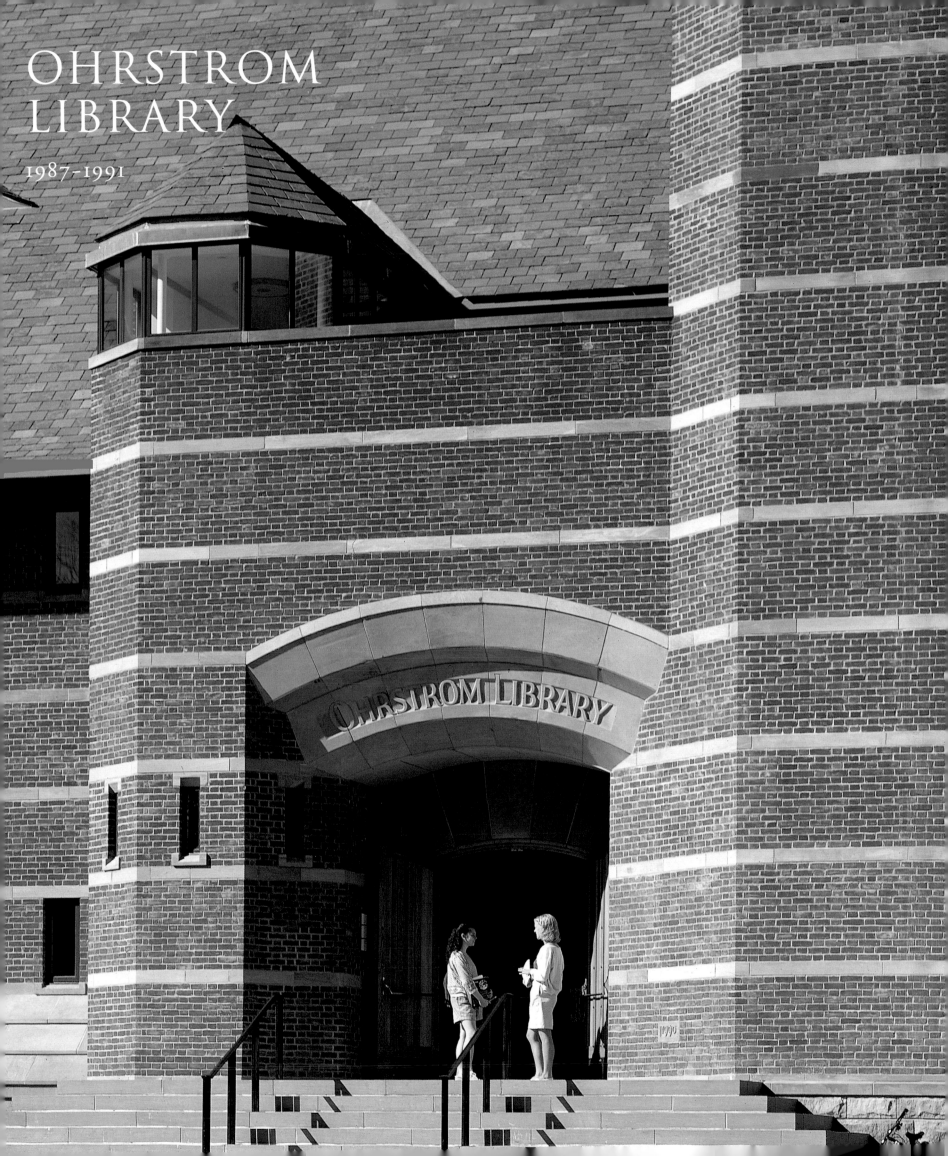

OHRSTROM
LIBRARY

1987-1991

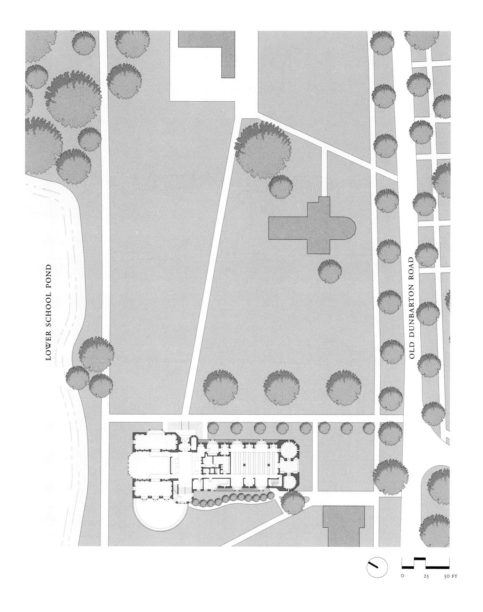

*West facade across
Lower School Pond.*

LOWER SCHOOL POND

OLD DUNBARTON ROAD

0   25   50 FT

THE CAM
AS CITAD

GEORGETOWN UNIVERSITY

WASHINGTON, D. C. Georgetown University has occupied a commanding site above the Potomac River since its founding in 1789 by John Carroll, then Archbishop of Baltimore. The first three university buildings, constructed in the Georgian style within six years of the school's establishment, were perched at the highest point overlooking the river, but they cannot be said to have been conceived as a citadel. Like those at the University of North Carolina at Chapel Hill, they were pavilions in a garden. Such was not the case after the Civil War when Smithmeyer & Pelz's Healy Hall (1879), its serious gray stone mass in stark contradiction to the modest red-brick Georgian past, assertively proclaimed the college's presence on the evolving skyline of the nation's capital.

university's Bicentennial Master Plan of 1989. Our job was to translate an abstract set of entitlements into a specific set of physical proposals for the university's future, especially as it realized new buildings on precious open land that extended up from the river to the campus plateau.

Georgetown's Southwest Quadrangle (2003), the first phase of the 1992 master plan, fills in part of the valley lying west of the campus bluff with a new quadrangle consisting of three independent but attached six- to eight-story residence halls that share a variety of ground floor social facilities, a Jesuit residence designed by Einhorn Yaffee Prescott, and, as its focal component, our Leo J. O'Donovan Hall, a 1,200-seat dining facility that provides dramatic views over the Potomac River.

In the first half of the twentieth century, Georgetown grew slowly, but following World War II, it exploded in size, with stylistically diverse buildings that seemed to have in common only a rejection of what had come before. One or two aimed higher: Hugh Newell Jacobsen's Alumni Square (1983) was a serious attempt to relate to the residential context of the adjacent neighborhood.

In 1992 we were asked to develop a ten-year implementation plan to be based on the

GEORGETOWN UNIVERSITY
CAMPUS PLAN

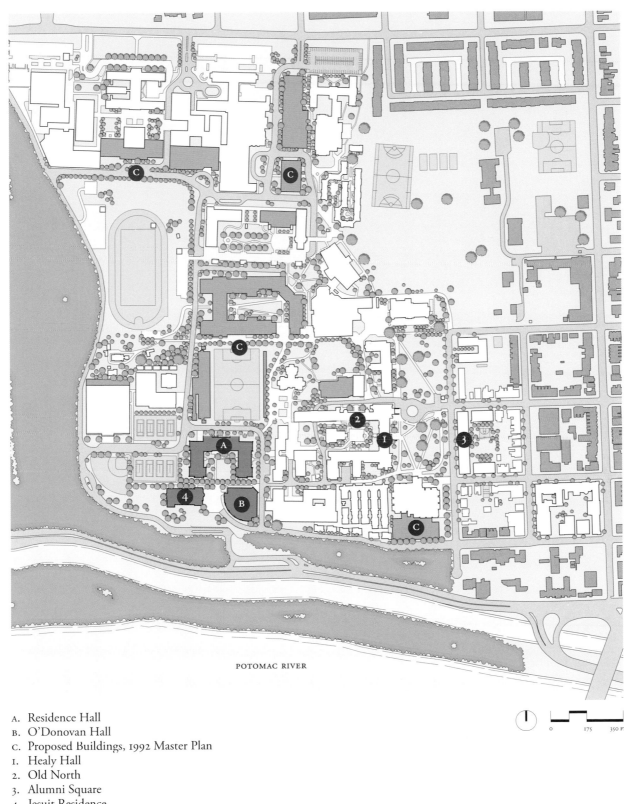

POTOMAC RIVER

A. Residence Hall
B. O'Donovan Hall
C. Proposed Buildings, 1992 Master Plan
1. Healy Hall
2. Old North
3. Alumni Square
4. Jesuit Residence

0   175   350 FT

LEFT
*View looking south
through breezeway at
Kennedy Hall.*

RIGHT
*O'Donovan Hall from
Library Walk.*

TRINITY UNIVERSITY

SAN ANTONIO, TEXAS. Originally founded in 1869 in Tehuacana, Texas, on a site six miles from the nearest railroad station that appealed to the founders' desire for isolation, in 1902 Trinity moved to Waxahachie, a rail hub south of Dallas, and then to the west side of San Antonio in 1942. In 1952 the university moved once again, this time to a 107-acre site atop a bluff overlooking San Antonio, where it established a "skyline campus," planned by O'Neil Ford, whose functionalist buildings, adapting brick, metal, and glass to the city's subtropical climate, are a showpiece of regionally responsive modernism.

NORTHRUP HALL

2000–2004

LEFT
Main stair.

RIGHT
Upper lobby.

COLLEGE OF NOTRE DAME OF MARYLAND

BALTIMORE, MARYLAND. The College of Notre Dame of Maryland, the first Roman Catholic college for women in the United States, was founded in 1873 as the Notre Dame Collegiate Institute for Young Ladies, moving shortly after its establishment from cramped quarters in Baltimore to a ruralesque neighborhood dotted by large country estates. The college's first purpose-built home, Gibbons Hall (1873), crowning a hill overlooking Baltimore, was intended to be the centerpiece of a much larger structure.

Like Georgetown's Healy Hall, Gibbons was dramatically situated along the crest of a hill to function as a citadel of learning. Its robust, northern European-derived vocabulary was not only fashionable, but also appropriate to the German origins of the college's founding order, the School Sisters of Notre Dame.

Gibbons and its annex (now Theresa Hall) served the college well for a generation, but when it came time to expand facilities in the new century the college chose to build a freestanding building. College Hall (1911), a multi-purpose Italianate palazzo, was sited below the hill in order to directly confront Charles Street, a major Baltimore artery, suggesting a shift in institutional identity from aloof superiority to engaged cosmopolitanism.

Other buildings followed, but in the 1950s, almost all sense of institutional identity or coherence gave way to a bland functionalism amid a planning jumble. Our master plan for the college (1997) reorganized roads and parking to create a formal College Walk and to make room for expanded sports fields as well as a number of new buildings and additions. We subsequently realized a 40,000-square-foot addition (2000) to the dreary Knott Science Center, providing state-of-the-art laboratories, support space, classrooms, and offices, as well as a dignified entrance to what was, at best, a workhorse building from the 1960s. Stylistically, the new wing refers to the Gothic of Gibbons Hall, the college's first building and still its most important.

COLLEGE OF NOTRE DAME OF MARYLAND
CAMPUS PLAN

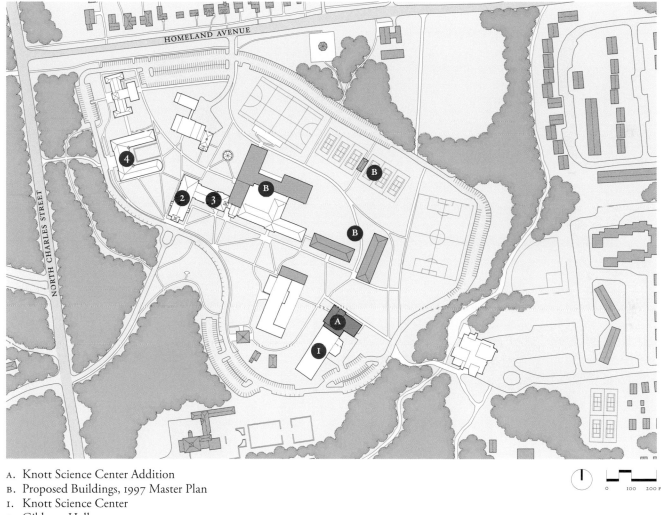

A. Knott Science Center Addition
B. Proposed Buildings, 1997 Master Plan
1. Knott Science Center
2. Gibbons Hall
3. Theresa Hall
4. College Hall

KNOTT SCIENCE
CENTER ADDITION

1997–2000

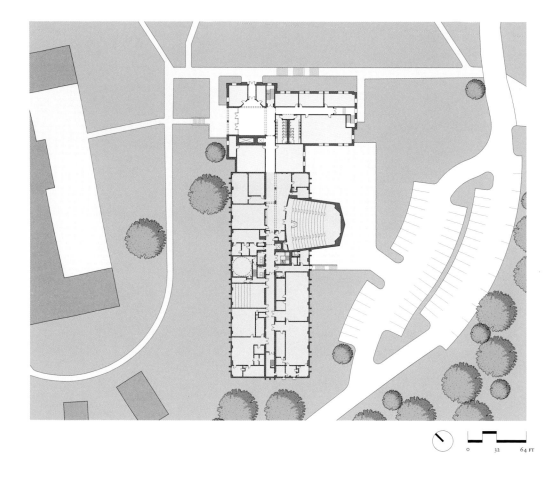

ROBERT A.M. STERN: ON CAMPUS

FRED VOGELSTEIN '80   JOHN L. VOGELSTEIN '52 DORMITORY

THE TAFT SCHOOL

WATERTOWN, CONNECTICUT. In 1890 Horace Dutton Taft, a Yale-trained educator, was invited by a family friend to head a new college preparatory school for boys to be located in Pelham Manor, New York. After two years, Taft sought a location farther from New York City, and in 1893 the nascent school, by then called "Mr. Taft's School," moved to Watertown, Connecticut. There, with a ten-thousand-dollar loan, Taft and his new wife, Winifred, set up shop in a former hotel despite parental fears that the woodframe building was a "firetrap" with drinking water of dubious quality.

The school prospered and the Tafts envisioned a proper campus to be built some two miles away on land they owned on Nova Scotia Hill, commissioning the New York firm of Cram, Goodhue & Ferguson to prepare plans. But the project was abandoned when Mrs. Taft became ill, and, beginning in 1908, the school was redeveloped facing the Watertown Green according to plans by Bertram Grosvenor Goodhue, who designed a single picturesquely massed Gothic building combining living, educational, and recreational facilities. Although not perched on a hilltop, Taft was nonetheless a citadel of learning.

Three years after Goodhue's death in 1924, when the school needed to double its facilities, Taft's trustees turned to James Gamble Rogers, who had also taken over for Goodhue at Yale.

Rogers extended Goodhue's planning strategy as well as the Gothic language and red brick vocabulary of the original building, arraying a mixture of uses along a system of corridors leading from a spatially inventive stair hall.

However, when new facilities were required in the 1960s, the school not only turned away from the single building approach with its mixture of uses, but also from romantic medievalism, so that both the Mathematics and Science Building (1962) and the Hulbert Taft Jr. Library (1968) were designed in a modernist aesthetic as freestanding facilities.

In 1994, we were invited to participate in a competition for a new Mathematics and Science Building, intended as a first step in a phased strategy that would allow the school not only to significantly improve its facilities but also to re-embrace its now-compromised architectural identity. Our proposal was not accepted, but five years later we were given the opportunity to realize the John L. Vogelstein '52 Dormitory (2002), a new residence hall directly connected to Rogers's Charles Phelps Taft Hall (1929). Housing forty-eight students in single rooms arranged into two-room suites, as well as faculty apartments, four common rooms, and three classrooms, Vogelstein adds to Rogers's work as Rogers added to Goodhue's, contributing new thoughts to a shared formal language.

RIGHT
Horace Dutton Taft Hall, Bertram Grosvenor Goodhue, 1913.

MIDDLE
Charles Phelps Taft Hall, James Gamble Rogers, 1929.

BELOW
Hulbert Taft Jr. Library, Jeter & Cook, 1968.

THE TAFT SCHOOL
CAMPUS PLAN

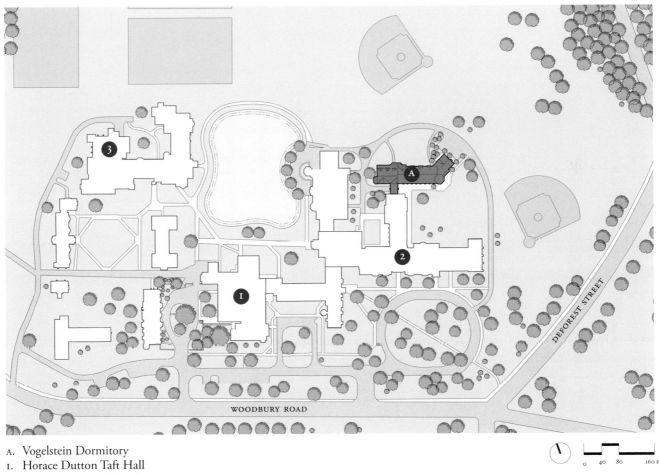

A. Vogelstein Dormitory
1. Horace Dutton Taft Hall
2. Charles Phelps Taft Hall
3. Library

VOGELSTEIN
DORMITORY

1999–2002

PREVIOUS PAGES
*View looking northwest
with Charles Phelps
Taft Hall (James Gamble
Rogers, 1929) at left.*

RIGHT
Arcade bridge.

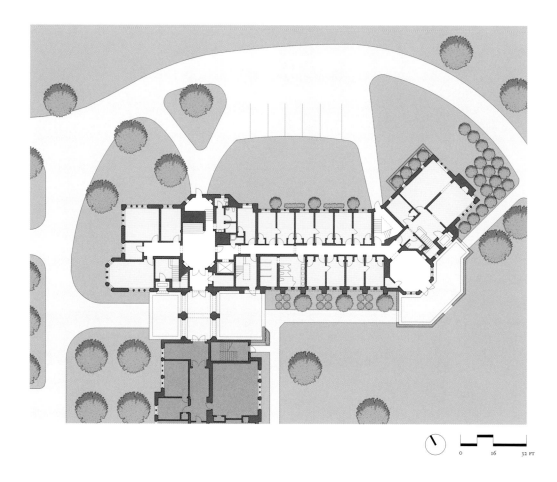

0   16   32 FT

ITHACA COLLEGE

ITHACA, NEW YORK. Established in 1931 as an amalgam of smaller, vocation-specific institutes and schools, Ithaca College originally occupied a multitude of re-purposed spaces in downtown Ithaca, New York, while its Ivy League neighbor, Cornell, sprawled across high ground to its east. After years of imagining the possibilities of open fields commanding the southern end of Cayuga Lake, land was acquired and ground was broken for a new campus in 1960.

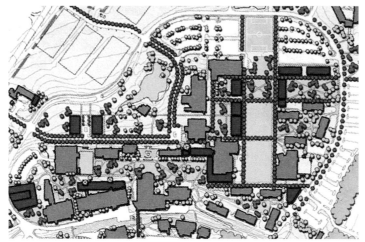

Ithaca College School of Business, occupies a central location in that plan, using a new courtyard, pedestrian bridge, and building entrances on two levels to help pedestrians negotiate the steep topography.

Showcasing Ithaca College's commitment to environmental responsibility, the Park Center's layered mass wraps various activities around a four-story atrium and a dramatic stair behind a south-facing curtain wall of glass, bringing direct and borrowed daylight to classrooms, study rooms, and offices. The building's abstract composition and detailing reflect the stylistic modernism of the college's other buildings, but its rubblestone base, garden terraces, and green roof engage with local landscape.

TOP
View to Cayuga Lake.

ABOVE
Master plan, Sasaki Associates, 2002.

RIGHT ABOVE
Ford Hall, Tallman & Tallman, 1964.

RIGHT BELOW
Friends Hall, Tallman & Tallman, 1963.

Regrettably, as this campus evolved, it tended to a somewhat inward-looking, muddled plan better suited to the circulation of automobiles than pedestrians across the commanding, but steeply sloping, site. A 2002 campus plan prepared by Sasaki Associates called for the development of three-sided quadrangles open to northern views across Cayuga Lake and for a broad landscaped mall running north to south across the site's steep slope. The Dorothy D. and Roy H. Park Center for Business and Sustainable Enterprise (2008), the new home for the

ITHACA COLLEGE
CAMPUS PLAN

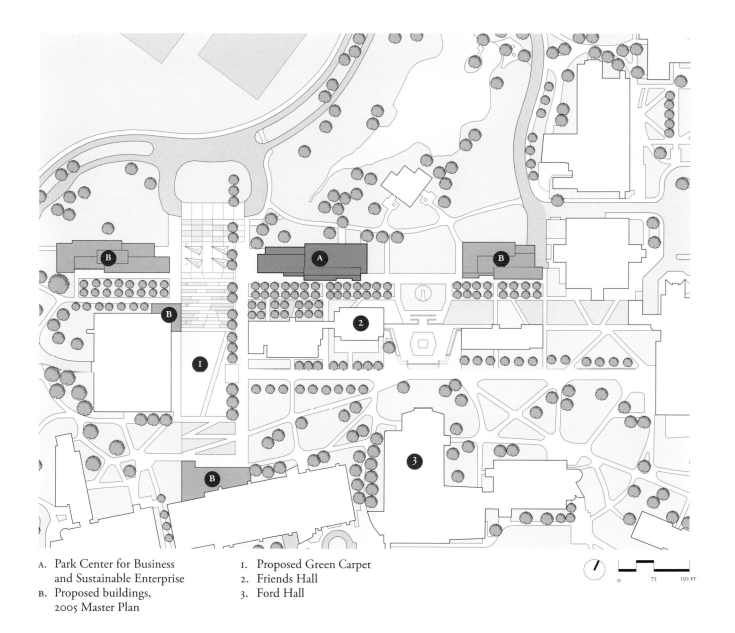

A. Park Center for Business
   and Sustainable Enterprise
B. Proposed buildings,
   2005 Master Plan

1. Proposed Green Carpet
2. Friends Hall
3. Ford Hall

PARK CENTER FOR BUSINESS AND SUSTAINABLE ENTERPRISE

ITHACA COLLEGE SCHOOL OF BUSINESS

2005–2008

LEFT
Atrium.

RIGHT TOP
*Atrium looking toward
moot boardroom.*

RIGHT BOTTOM
Moot boardroom.

THE GAR
CAMPUS

DEN

PAGES 484–485
*Harriet Irving Botanical
Gardens, Acadia
University.*

LEFT
Center for Jewish Life.

PRINCETON UNIVERSITY

PRINCETON, NEW JERSEY. The founders of the College of New Jersey appear to have anticipated the metropolitan crisis very early on: in 1752 they moved their fledgling institution, not renamed Princeton University until 1896, from a room above the Newark jail to a country village that the trustees found "more sequestered from the various temptations attending a promiscuous commerce with the world, that theatre of folly and dissipation."[1] Furthermore, the trustees set Nassau Hall (1755–57), the main building of the relocated institution, far back from the road amid eleven acres—creating the first leafy setting for collegiate life to be called by the name "campus," meaning field in Latin, and in so doing putting a name to a uniquely American phenomenon.[2]

At Princeton the idea of campus as field held a specific meaning describing a type of community significantly different from its immediate collegiate predecessors. Princeton developed neither as a counterbalancing part of a town as did William and Mary, nor as a series of "yards" embedded in a town as at Harvard and Yale. Nor was Princeton a self-contained village such as Jefferson would realize at Charlottesville. At first, as in the white clapboard of Whig and Clio halls (1838, rebuilt in 1893), Greek temples opposite Nassau Hall, the feeling was not so different, let us say, from that of Stowe, in England. The pattern of gardenesque scattering continued after the Civil War, when William Appleton Potter set Princeton's architecture in

a very different stylistic direction, abandoning provincial classicism for rugged individualism, with the octagonal Chancellor Green Library (1873) evoking Venice and the hulking Alexander Hall (1892) suggesting medieval France. Bounded space remained anathema at Princeton until classics professor Andrew F. West, who would later become dean of the Graduate School, took the celebrations of the college's sesquicentennial in 1896 as an opportunity to put an end to Princeton's stylistic eclecticism. Intent on persuading the trustees that along with transforming the sleepy college into a university, Princeton needed to put its architectural house in order, West argued that the new university would most easily become a great and venerable institution if it looked like one, specifically if it looked like Oxford or Cambridge.

But West did not advocate that Princeton completely abandon its essential characteristic as a "garden campus." Rather, he and his architects, notably Cope & Stewardson, followed by Ralph Adams Cram and others, realized a succession of loosely arrayed groups casually situated in the landscape, including the Graduate College (1913), arguably one of

the most beautiful "Gothic" quadrangles ever constructed, located not on a site mediating between the bustle of village streets and the "backs" such as was the case at Oxford and Cambridge, but situated in splendid isolation, approached from the main campus across a meticulously landscaped golf course.

Our role in the story of Princeton's architectural evolution is not much more than a footnote. In 1986 we were invited to provide a permanent home for the newly instituted Center for Jewish Life accommodating a worship hall and social spaces by expanding an 1896 private residence that had subsequently housed undergraduate eating clubs. The initial scheme called for renovating the house and adding wings to either side to accommodate the Center's program.

ABOVE
Chancellor Green Library, William Appleton Potter, 1873.

LEFT
Alexander Hall, William Appleton Potter, 1892.

BELOW
Graduate College, Ralph Adams Cram, 1913.

But when the old house proved structurally unsound, an entirely new building was realized based on the original parti. Taking cues from the Arts and Crafts manner of the original house, the Center for Jewish Life (1993) takes advantage of its corner site, locating the formal entrance on Washington Avenue on the west but opening its broad side to Ivy Lane on the south where the downward slope allows for a sun-splashed terrace, linked to a garden by a broad flight of steps.

1. Princeton trustees, quoted in Alexander Leitch, *A Princeton Companion* (Princeton, N.J.: Princeton University Press, 1978), 75.
2. Leitch, 74; Paul Venable Turner, *Campus: An American Planning Tradition* (New York: The Architectural History Foundation, and Cambridge, Mass.: The MIT Press, 1984), 47.

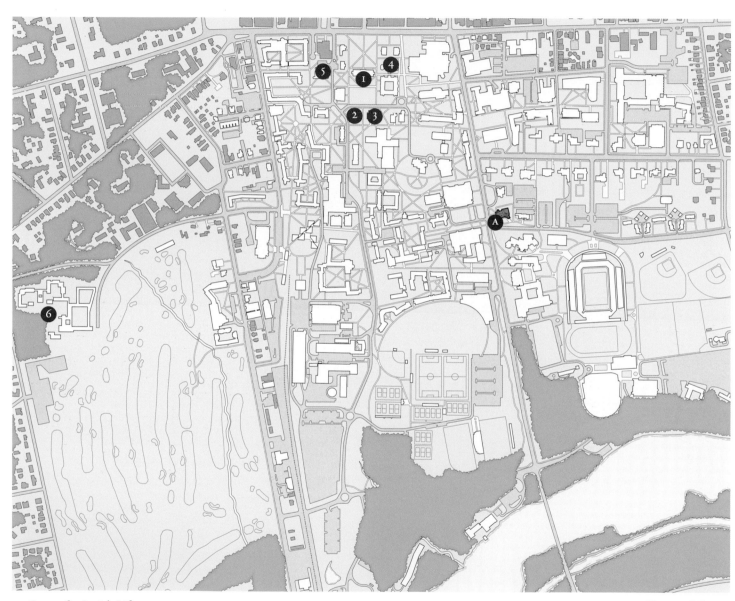

A. Center for Jewish Life
1. Nassau Hall
2. Clio Hall
3. Whig Hall
4. Chancellor Green Library
5. Alexander Hall
6. Graduate Quad

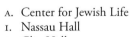

CENTER FOR
JEWISH LIFE

1986–1993

LEFT TOP
Dining hall.

LEFT BOTTOM
Library.

RIGHT
Sanctuary.

UNIVERSITY OF NORTH CAROLINA

CHAPEL HILL, NORTH CAROLINA. Arguably the first state-supported university, the University of North Carolina at Chapel Hill adopted a plan in 1792 that, on the one hand, echoed the evolved physical relationship of the College of William and Mary to the town of Williamsburg, and on the other, reflected the prejudice against towns that Thomas Jefferson was to underscore in planning the University of Virginia.

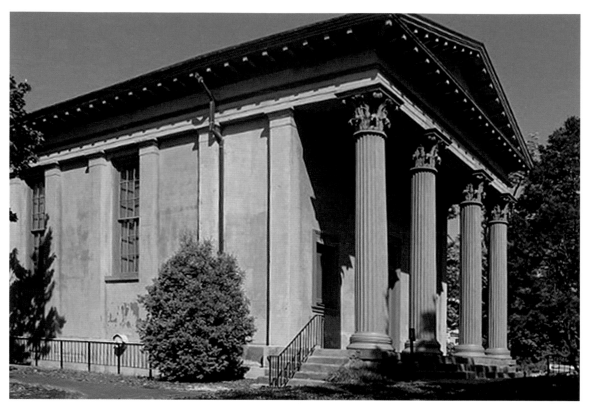

ABOVE
Smith Hall, Alexander Jackson Davis, 1850.

BELOW
Plan for the University and town lots, 1795.

As planned, the new college and its college town were originally to form a single entity, with three connected academic buildings proposed for the end of a "grand avenue," in effect a landscaped mall flanked by house lots, ironically a strategy that contained the seeds of Jefferson's plan for the University of Virginia. But the grand avenue was never realized, and as the college grew, like Princeton, it loosely grouped disconnected and widely spaced buildings to form open quadrangles floating in the landscape.

In 1848 Alexander Jackson Davis, one of the country's leading architects, expanded the three original buildings, overlaying their raw, meant-for-business utilitarianism with a sparing use of architectural rhetoric—a tetrastyle portico added to Gerrard Hall (1837), a pediment-inspired expression for the gabled end of Smith Hall (1850) carried on piers—to enhance what Montgomery Schuyler called "the signalization of the entrance."[1] In 1921 McKim, Mead & White, then led by William Kendall, was called in to help with the university's expansion.

With its characteristic sensitivity to context, the firm carried forward reinterpretations of Davis's early work with new buildings such as Saunders, Manning, and Murphy Halls (1923) forming a new quadrangle.

As the university grew, the campus expanded to the south well beyond its original bounds, where Arthur Cleveland Nash, who succeeded McKim, Mead & White, successfully realized

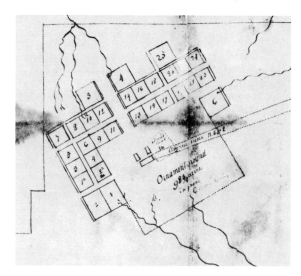

dormitory quadrangles echoing the earliest campus buildings, and, at a bold new scale, Kenan Stadium (1927), one of the icons of collegiate football. But in 1963, Kenan was savaged by an addition praised for its open concrete framework recalling "bleachers at the circus or high school athletic fields back home" served by "two spiral ramps marking the entrance," used "like monumental sculptures, lifting the crowd in body and spirit."[2] Other additions followed, visually obliterating Nash's original structure and swamping the garden campus with an aggressive mass. In 2008, as yet another expansion to Kenan was being contemplated, in this case to provide much-needed restrooms and concession spaces at the concourse level and an academic training center above, we proposed to wrap the structure in a layer of tall brick arcades that would visually restate Nash's

original intentions and thereby reconnect it with the architectural character of the adjacent historic campus.

As the UNC campus has expanded, its never-very-clear plan of roads and paths has become ever more muddled, making the need for clearly defined pedestrian pathways connecting outlying buildings with the historic core ever more apparent. Our Student and Academic Services Buildings (2007), two three-story buildings housing a variety of student services previously dispersed around the campus, constitute a node of pedestrian activity at a key intersection of roads in the south part of the campus. The use of red brick, with oversized wood windows and a metal roof, extends the language of the historic core, recalling in particular the work of Davis, whose renovations of UNC's original buildings helped lift them from mere utilitarianism into the realm of architecture.

ABOVE
Proposed Kenan Stadium expansion, Robert A. M. Stern Architects, 2008.

LEFT
Old West, with alterations by Alexander Jackson Davis, 1844.

BELOW
Manning and Murphy Halls, McKim, Mead & White, 1923.

1. Montgomery Schuyler, "Architecture of American Colleges VIII— The Southern Colleges," *Architectural Record* 30 (July 1911): 64.
2. John V. Alcott, *The Campus at Chapel Hill: Two Hundred Years of Architecture,* (Chapel Hill, N.C.: The Chapel Hill Historical Society, 1986), 77.

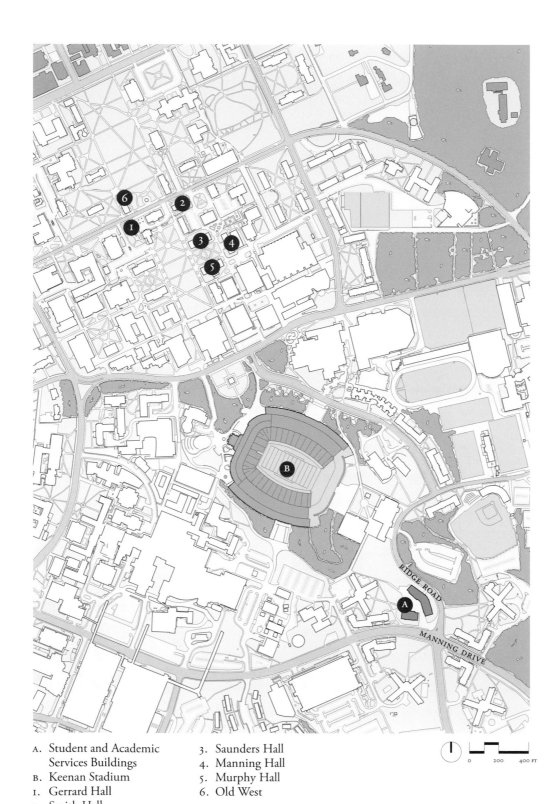

A. Student and Academic
   Services Buildings
B. Keenan Stadium
1. Gerrard Hall
2. Smith Hall

3. Saunders Hall
4. Manning Hall
5. Murphy Hall
6. Old West

STUDENT
AND ACADEMIC
SERVICES
BUILDINGS

2004–2007

Entrance to north building.

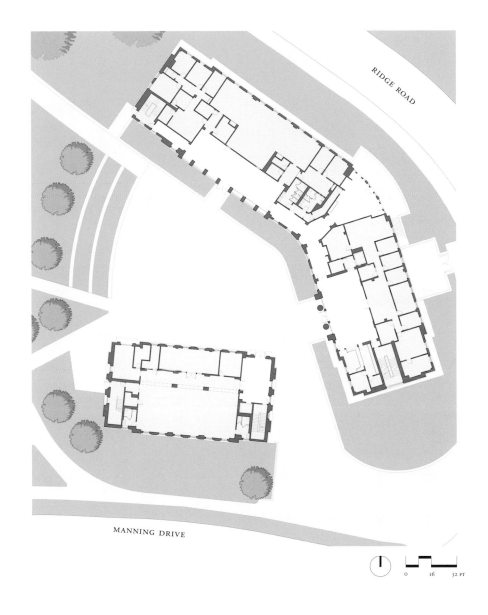

RIDGE ROAD

MANNING DRIVE

0   16   32 FT

PENNSYLVANIA STATE UNIVERSITY

STATE COLLEGE, PENNSYLVANIA. Founded as the Farmers' School in 1855 on 400 acres of isolated land ideal for the study of the agricultural sciences, Penn State was initially housed in a single structure, a strategy that was typical of many other newly established educational institutions in the mid-nineteenth century. By the twentieth century, the former agricultural school was well on its way to becoming a major university. However, despite efforts in 1907 by Charles N. Lowrie, a landscape architect from New York, and in 1914 by Charles Z. Klauder, a Philadelphia-based architect specializing in college buildings, its campus lacked clear planning definition.

Klauder did his best to give Penn State an architectural identity, replacing the structurally unsound original Main Building with a new one in 1930. The Georgian-style building commands a spacious landscaped mall leading from "front gates" facing South Main Street where the campus borders the town of College Station, much as Princeton's Nassau Hall looks across a greensward to Princeton Borough.

In the post–World War II era, the campus grew exponentially to the north and east, challenging Old Main's focal status. Recently, as a result of new freeway construction, the campus has developed a second "front door" facing Park Avenue, which has become the principal point of arrival for visitors. In response, the combined crescent of the new home of the Smeal College of Business Administration (2005) and the adjacent home of the School of Forest Resources, designed by Bower Lewis Thrower (2006), were conceived together to constitute a second gateway for the university and to frame a new mall penetrating deep into the campus. The composition of Smeal and to a lesser extent its smaller companion reflects the arrangement of Eero Saarinen's Morse and Stiles Colleges at Yale, with intimate courtyards behind a bold crescent. At Smeal, the courtyard is linked to a boldly scaled light-flooded multi-level commons that constitutes a social mixing venue for the business school's graduate and undergraduate students, faculty, and staff.

PENNSYLVANIA STATE UNIVERSITY
CAMPUS PLAN

A. Smeal College of Business
B. Garage and Chiller Plant
1. Old Main
2. Agricultural Sciences
3. School of Forest Resources

SMEAL COLLEGE
OF BUSINESS
ADMINISTRATION

2001–2005

BUSINESS
BUILDING

EAST PARK AVENUE

SHORTLIDGE ROAD

0   32   64 FT

ACADIA
UNIVERSITY

WOLFVILLE, NOVA SCOTIA, CANADA. Situated at the head of the Bay of Fundy, Acadia University, a small liberal arts university founded in 1839, had by the 1930s become an attractive garden campus. Sadly, following World War II, Acadia entered a period characterized by a lack of planning and generally lowered architectural standards, attributable, at least in part, to the imposition of government control over all Canadian institutions of higher education.

IRVING ENVIRONMENTAL SCIENCE CENTRE AND BOTANICAL GARDENS

1998–2002

MARIST COLLEGE

POUGHKEEPSIE, NEW YORK. Established in 1905 as a seminary atop a bluff facing the Hudson River, Marist became a fully accredited college in 1946. Its facilities were housed in picturesque Hudson River Gothic villas augmented by sparely detailed academic buildings and residence halls designed and often constructed by the Marist Brothers. Recently, the college has grown dramatically, following a loose plan that reorganizes the campus around a variety of open spaces that complement the site's extraordinary topography, with our Hancock Technology Center its critical linchpin.

MARIST COLLEGE
CAMPUS PLAN

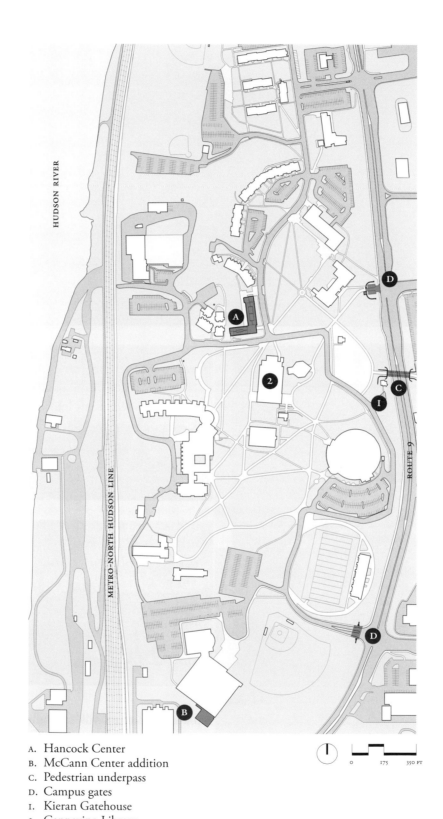

A. Hancock Center
B. McCann Center addition
C. Pedestrian underpass
D. Campus gates
1. Kieran Gatehouse
2. Cannavino Library

0   175   350 FT

HANCOCK TECHNOLOGY CENTER

2007–2011

CALIFORNIA STATE UNIVERSITY NORTHRIDGE

NORTHRIDGE, CALIFORNIA. When the campus of California State University Northridge opened as a community college in 1956, the San Fernando Valley, which had been a landscape of ranches and rural towns until World War II, was quickly being transformed into a satellite community of Los Angeles. The first wave of college construction on the 165-acre site brought with it little of architectural distinction. In the 1960s and 1970s several buildings, including a decidedly pompous signature building, Oviatt Library (1973), were constructed around a large quadrangle in an attempt to provide a center amid the sprawl.

One building struggled to rise above the general blandness: Richard Neutra's interesting, L-shaped Fine Arts Building (1959).

The Northridge earthquake in January 1994 damaged virtually all the university's buildings, some irreparably, including Neutra's, which was particularly hard hit. A 1998 master plan led to the decision to replace the Fine Arts Building with our Manzanita Hall (2001), providing a new home for the College of Arts, Media, and Communication.

Manzanita Hall addresses Sierra Quad, the principal open space on campus, with a triple-height roofed entrance loggia behind which lies a 120-seat screening room. Two-story-high glass-walled art galleries sheltered by an upward curving roof, carried on a double-height colonnade of tripartite metal column bundles, constitute the building's public face to the university. Stretching to the west and south behind the glass and brick facade, a stucco-clad

L-shaped mass defining two sides of a landscaped green accommodates offices, classrooms, and studios.

CALIFORNIA STATE
UNIVERSITY, NORTHRIDGE
CAMPUS PLAN

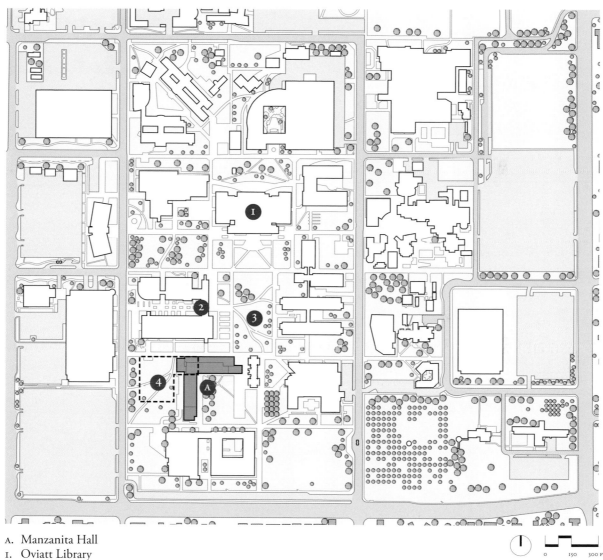

A. Manzanita Hall
1. Oviatt Library
2. Sierra Hall
3. Sierra Quad
4. Fine Arts Building by Richard Neutra

0   150   300 FT

MANZANITA HALL

MIKE CURB COLLEGE OF ARTS,
MEDIA, AND COMMUNICATION
1997-2001

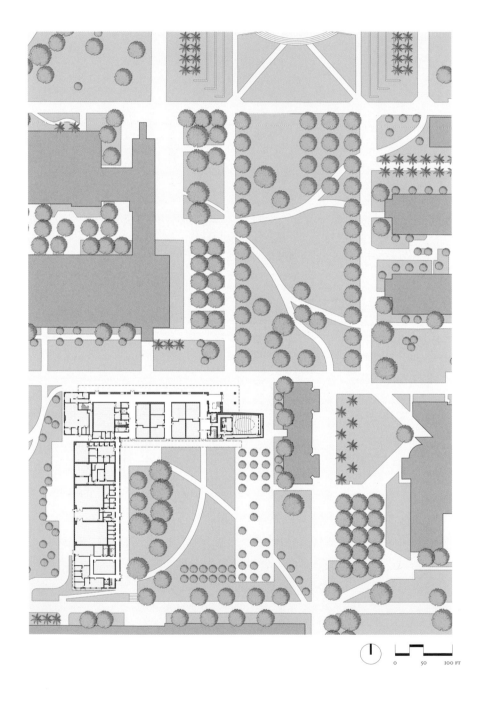

LEFT
Grand stair at upper hall.

RIGHT TOP
Classroom.

RIGHT BOTTOM
Screening room.

UNIVERSITY OF NEVADA, LAS VEGAS

LAS VEGAS, NEVADA. A virtual anomaly within a commercial city that has yet to develop a significant public realm of institutions, the Las Vegas campus of the University of Nevada has since 1957 occupied an 80-acre site a short distance from the Strip. Mirroring the rapid and haphazard growth of its host city, the campus is squeezed between two major arterials in the ever-growing pattern of sprawl. Hardly a garden, the Las Vegas campus nonetheless shares with the garden type a fundamental characteristic: a loose plan. The evolution of the campus of UNLV is clearly at a point of transition. As it grows and sites are filled in, it may crystallize as an embedded campus, offering—to some extent, given its surroundings—a sense of Jeffersonian isolation, if not necessarily repose or architectural didacticism.

GREENSPUN HALL

GREENSPUN COLLEGE OF URBAN AFFAIRS

2005-2008

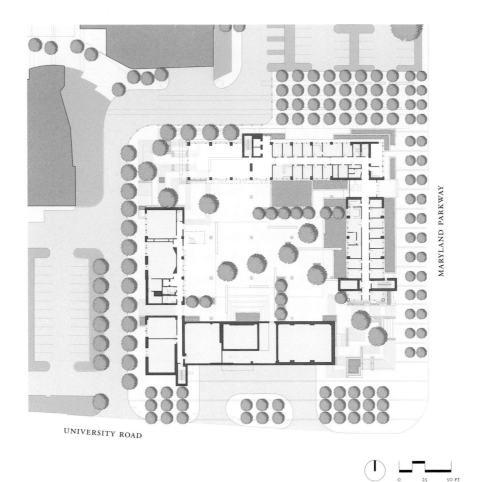

MARYLAND PARKWAY

UNIVERSITY ROAD

0   25   50 FT

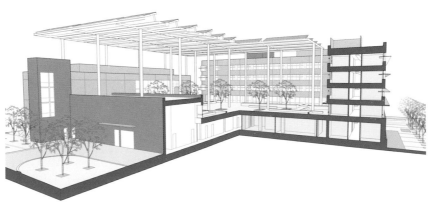

CUT-AWAY VIEW

LEFT TOP
Upper lounge.

LEFT BOTTOM
Lobby.

RIGHT
*View to courtyard from
upper-floor corridor.*

OVERLEAF
Courtyard looking north.

Kathleen Mancini-Ferrigno. Associate Architect: CO Architects (formerly Anshen + Allen Los Angeles). Landscape Architect: Pamela Burton & Company.

Dartmouth College, Hanover, New Hampshire
Moore Psychology Building
Partner: Graham S. Wyatt. Project Architect: Preston J. Gumberich. Associates: Adam Anuszkiewicz, Augusta Barone. Senior Assistant: Meghan McDermott. Assistants: Elizabeth Adams, Ricardo Alvarez-Diaz, Frank de Santis, Shannon Gallagher, Jonas Goldberg, Claudia Lin, Quincey Nixon, Richard Schneider. Interior Design Assistants: Peter Fleming, Damion Phillips, Claire Ratliff. Landscape Architect: Rolland-Towers.

Miami University, Oxford, Ohio
Farmer School of Business
Partners: Preston J. Gumberich, Graham S. Wyatt. Senior Associate: Jeffery Povero. Associate: George Punnoose. Project Manager: Sean Foley. Assistants: Daniel Arbelaez, Afzal Hossain, Jill Lagowski, Michael Ryan, Yok Saowasang, Jeremy Shannon, Michael Tabacinic, Rob Teeters. Interior Design Associate: Shannon Ratcliff. Interior Design Assistants: Michelle Everett, Taylor Stein. Associate Architect: Moody Nolan. Landscape Architect: James Burkart Associates.

St. Paul's School, Concord, New Hampshire
Ohrstrom Library
Project Architect: Graham S. Wyatt. Project Managers: Preston Gumberich, Caryl Kinsey. Associate: Charles D. Warren. Assistants: Abigail M. Huffman, Timothy Lenahan, Sandra Parsons, Sharon Pett, Eva Pohlen, Mary Ellen Stenger. Interior Design Associate: Lisa Maurer. Interior Design Assistant: Alice Yiu. Landscape Design Associate: Robert Ermerins. Landscape Design Assistant: William Skelsey.

THE CAMPUS AS CITADEL

Georgetown University, Washington, D. C.
Southwest Quadrangle
Partner: Graham S. Wyatt. Senior Assistants: Frank de Santis, Jonilla Dorsten, Dana Gulling, Rebecca Laubach, Kevin O'Connor. Assistants: Marina Berendeeva, Laura Hinton, Edwin Hofmann, James Johnson, Dewi Jones, Antonio Ng, Sung Ok, James Park, Jong-Hyuck Park, Lenore Passavanti, Christopher Podstawski, Anthony Polito, Corina Rugeroni, Katherine Snow, Karina Tengberg, John Ullman, Michael Wilbur, Yuri Zagorin, Paul Zamek, Sandra Zenk. Landscape Design Associate: Dawn Handler. Landscape Design Assistants: Peter Arato, Norbert Holter, John Merritt, Eric Samuels. Interior Design Senior Associate: John Gilmer. Interior Design Assistant: Paola Velazquez. Associate Architect: Einhorn Yaffee Prescott. Landscape Architect: Stephenson & Good.

Trinity University, San Antonio, Texas
Northrup Hall
Partner: Alexander P. Lamis. Senior Associate: Adam Anuszkiewicz. Associates: Diane Burkin, Enid De Gracia, Thomas Fletcher, Salvador Peña-Figueroa. Project Manager: Mike Soriano. Assistants: Julia

Buse, Ernesto Martinez, Ahmad-ali Sardar-Afkhami. Interior Design Associate: Hyung Kee Lee. Interior Design Assistants: Virginia Cornell, Kathleen Mancini. Landscape Design Project Manager: Ashley Christopher. Associate Architect: Kell Muñoz Architects.

College of Notre Dame of Maryland, Baltimore, Maryland
Knott Science Center Addition
Partner: Graham S. Wyatt. Associate: Augusta Barone. Assistants: James Johnson, Dennis Sagiev. Landscape Design Assistant: Ann Stokes. Associate Architect: George Vaeth Associates.

The Taft School, Watertown, Connecticut
Vogelstein Dormitory
Partner: Graham S. Wyatt. Senior Associate: Jeffery Povero. Project Manager: Malaika Kim. Senior Assistants: John Cays, Ed Leveckis. Assistants: Gordon Cousins, Elise Geiger, Don Johnson, Scott Kruger, Jonathan Toews. Interior Design Senior Associate: John Gilmer. Interior Design Assistants: Vennie Lau, Ken Stuckenschneider, Joy Tucci. Landscape Design Assistants: Norbert Holter, Sung Ok. Landscape Architect: Ann P. Stokes Landscape Architects.

Ithaca College, Ithaca, New York
Park Center for Business and Sustainable Enterprise
Partners: Kevin M. Smith, Graham S. Wyatt. Senior Associates: Dennis Sagiev, Jennifer Stone. Associate: Sue Jin Sung. Assistants: Roland Sharpe Flores, Lorenzo Galati, Natalie Goldberg, Lara Kailian, Eric Silinsh, Saul Uranovsky. Interior Design Associate: John Boyland. Interior Design Assistant: Leah Taylor. Landscape Architect: Hargreaves Associates.

THE GARDEN CAMPUS

Princeton University, Princeton, New Jersey
Center for Jewish Life
Project Architect: Alexander P. Lamis. Associate: Thomas A. Kligerman. Senior Assistants: Preston J. Gumberich, Lee Ledbetter. Assistants: Stephen Falatko, Alexis Fernandez, Abigail Huffman, Valerie Hughes, Arthur Platt, Pat Tiné, Elizabeth Valella.

University of North Carolina at Chapel Hill, Chapel Hill, North Carolina
Student and Academic Services Buildings
Partners: Kevin M. Smith, Graham S. Wyatt. Senior Associate: Melissa DelVecchio. Project Manager: Lara Kailian. Associate: Frederic Berthelot. Assistants: Lina Ayala, Gregory Christopher, Alex Pigott, Sue Jin Sung, Brian Taylor. Interior Design Associate: Shannon Ratcliff. Interior Design Assistant: Michelle Everett. Associate Architect: Corley Redfoot Zack. Landscape Architect: Ann P. Stokes Landscape Architect.

Pennsylvania State University, State College, Pennsylvania
Smeal College of Business
Partners: Kevin M. Smith, Graham S. Wyatt. Senior Associate: Jonas Goldberg. Associates: Frederic Berthelot, Enid De Gracia, Kevin Fitzgerald, Sue Jin

Sung. Senior Assistant: Gregory Christopher. Assistants: Jennifer Berlly, Alex Butler, Russell Greenberg, Jill Lagowski, Jennifer Newsom, Ryan Rodenberg, Lindsay Weiss. Associate Architect: Bower Lewis Thrower Architects. Landscape Architect: Lager Raabe Skafte, Sasaki Associates.

Acadia University, Wolfville, Nova Scotia, Canada
K.C. Irving Environmental Science Centre and Harriet Irving Botanical Gardens
Partner: Graham S. Wyatt. Senior Associate: Preston J. Gumberich. Associate: Geoffrey Mouen. Senior Assistant: Alex Karmeinsky. Assistants: Frederic Berthelot, John Cays, Elise Geiger, Jonas Goldberg, Breen Mahony, Antonio Ng, George Punnoose. Interior Design Assistants: Virginia Cornell, Amie Haugh, Vennie Lau, Scott Sloat. Associate Architect: Connor Architects & Planners. Associate Landscape Architect: Novell Tullett Landscape Architects.

Marist College, Poughkeepsie, New York
Hancock Technology Center
Partners: Kevin M. Smith, Graham S. Wyatt. Associate: Frederic Berthelot. Project Manager: Bram Janaitis. Project Architect: Michael Ryan. Senior Assistant: Celeste Hall. Assistants: Noel Angeles, Rebecca Atkin, Matthew Blumenthal, Isabel Gonzalez, Christopher Heim, Silas Jeffrey, Seema Malik, Ian Mills, Dongju Seo. Interior Design Project Manager: Phillip Chan. Interior Design Assistant: Tina Hu. Landscape Design Senior Associates: Kendra Taylor, Michael Weber. Landscape Design Project Manager: Mark Rodriguez. Landscape Design Assistants: Joelle Byrer, Meredith Lawton, Demetrios Staurinos.

California State University, Northridge, Northridge, California
Manzanita Hall, Mike Curb College of Arts, Media, and Communication
Partner: Alexander P. Lamis. Associate Partner: Barry Rice. Project Architect: Anselm Fusco. Assistants: Monique Agnew, Tricia Alvez, Frederic Berthelot, Frank Bostelmann, Arthur Chu, John Esposito, Matt Formicola, Zvi Gersh, Jennifer Hanlin, Stefan Mark Hare, Jae Kim, Nurcan Kisa, Mark Knoke, Nicole LaRossa, Candace Lee, Ernesto Leon, Andreas Paul Miller, Tamie Noponen, Rebecca Post, Nathan Quiring, Brock Roseberry, Heidi Sawyer, Samir Shah, Noah Shepherd, Ryan Sommers, Jonathan Toews, Aldona Tukallo, Michael Wilbur, Sandra Zenk. Landscape Design Associate: Dawn Handler. Landscape Design Assistant: Marie Andree Soundy. Interior Design Assistant: Damion Phillips. Associate Architect: Fields Devereaux Architects and Engineers.

University of Nevada, Las Vegas, Las Vegas, Nevada
Greenspun Hall, Greenspun College of Urban Affairs
Partners: Augusta Barone, Graham S. Wyatt. Senior Associate: Jeffery Povero. Assistants: Bradley Gay, Erin Murphy, Alicia Reed, Dongju Seo, Brian Stromquist, Michael Tabacinic. Interior Design Associate: Shannon Ratcliff. Interior Design Assistants: Michelle Everett, Marissa Savarese. Associate Architect: HKS. Landscape Architect: SWA Group.

BIBLIOGRAPHY

Alcott, John V. *The Campus at Chapel Hill: Two Hundred Years of Architecture.* Chapel Hill, N. C.: The Chapel Hill Historical Society, 1986.

Atterbury, Grosvenor, and Frederick Law Olmsted. *Report on the Physical Development of St. Paul's School: With Notes on Some of the Problems Connected Therewith, Past, Present and Future,* 1923.

Bezilla, Michael. *Penn State: An Illustrated History.* University Park, Pa., and London: The Pennsylvania State University Press, 1985.

Blodgett, Geoffrey. *Cass Gilbert: The Early Years.* St. Paul, Minn.: Minnesota Historical Society Press, 2001.

Boles, John B. *University Builder: Edgar Odell Lovett and the Founding of the Rice Institute.* Baton Rouge, La.: Louisiana State University Press, 2007.

Bordin, Ruth. *The University of Michigan: A Pictorial History.* Ann Arbor, Mich.: The University of Michigan Press, 1967.

Brown, Ian. "Irrelevance of University Architecture," *Architectural Forum* 136, no. 3 (April 1972): 50–55.

Bryan, John M. *An Architectural History of the South Carolina College, 1801–1855.* Columbia, S. C.: University of South Carolina Press, 1976.

———. *Robert Mills: America's First Architect.* New York: Princeton Architectural Press, 2001.

Buildings and Grounds of Yale University. New Haven: Yale University Printing Service, 1979.

Bunting, Bainbridge. *Harvard: An Architectural History.* Cambridge, Mass. and London: The Belknap Press of Harvard University Press, 1985.

Bush-Brown, Albert. *Image of a University: A Study of Architecture as an Expression of Education at Colleges and Universities in the United States between 1800 and 1900.* Princeton: Princeton University Press, 1958.

Christen, Barbara S., Steven Flanders, and Robert A. M. Stern, *Cass Gilbert: Life and Work. Architect of the Public Domain.* New York and London: W. W. Norton, 2001.

Cone, Carl B. *The University of Kentucky: A Pictorial History.* Lexington, Ky: The University Press of Kentucky, 1989.

Cram, Ralph Adams. "Have I a 'Philosophy of Design'?" *Pencil Points* 13 (November 1932).

Cruikshank, Jeffrey L. *A Delicate Experiment: The Harvard Business School 1900–1945.* Boston: Harvard University Press, 1987.

Dallasights: An Anthology of Architecture and Open Spaces. AIA Dallas, 1978.

Day, Douglas, and Douglas Llewellyn. *The Academical Village: Thomas Jefferson's University.* Charlottesville, Va.: Thomasson-Grant, 1982.

Deno, William R. *Body and Soul: Architectural Style at the University of Colorado at Boulder.* Boulder, Colo: University of Colorado at Boulder Publications Service, 1994.

Dillon, David. *The Architecture of O'Neil Ford: Celebrating Place.* Austin, Tex.: University of Texas Press, 1999.

Dorsey, John. *Look Again in Baltimore.* Baltimore: The Johns Hopkins University Press, 2005.

Duany, Andres. "Southern Discomfort." *Architecture* 90, no. 5 (May 2001): p176.

Dunwell, Steve. *Yale: A Portrait.* New Haven: The Office of the Secretary, Yale University, 1990.

———. *Harvard: A Living Portrait.* Boston: Back Bay Press, 1995.

Drexler, Arthur, and Thomas S. Hines. *The Architecture of Richard Neutra From International Style to California Modern.* New York: The Museum of Modern Art, 1982.

Eisdorfer, Erica, ed. *Carolina: Photographs from the First State University.* Chapel Hill, N. C.: The University of North Carolina Press, 2006.

Fox, Stephen. "The General Plan of the William M. Rice Institute and Its Architectural Development," *Architecture at Rice,* monograph 29, 1980.

———. *Rice University: The Campus Guide.* New York: Princeton Architectural Press, 2001.

Gaines, Thomas A. *The Campus as a Work of Art.* Westport, Conn., and London: Praeger, 1991.

George, Mary Carolyn Hollers. *O'Neil Ford, Architect.* College Station. Tex.: Texas A&M University Press, 1992.

Grieff, Constance M., Mary W. Gibbons, and Elizabeth G.C. Menzies. *Princeton Architecture: A Pictorial History of Town and Campus.* Princeton: Princeton University Press, 1967.

Hamlin, A. D. F. "Recent American College Architecture," *Outlook* 74, no. 14 (August 1, 1903): 790–99.

Harth, Marjorie L. *Pomona College: Reflections on a Campus.* Claremont, Calif.: Pomona College, 2007.

Havighurst, Walter. *The Miami Years, 1809–1984.* New York: G. P. Putnam's Sons, 1958.

Heckscher, August. *St. Paul's: The Life of a New England School.* New York: Charles Scribner's Sons, 1980.

Henry, Jay C. *Architecture in Texas: 1895–1945.* Austin, Tex.: University of Texas Press, 1993.

Hines, Thomas S. *Richard Neutra and the Search for Modern Architecture.* New York: Rizzoli, 2005.

Hogan, Pendleton. *The Lawn: A Guide to Jefferson's University.* Charlottesville, Va.: University Press of Virginia, 1987.

Holden, Rueben A. *Yale: A Pictorial History.* New Haven and London: Yale University Press, 1967.

Hope, Arthur J., C.S.C. *Notre Dame: One Hundred Years* (second ed.). Notre Dame, Ind.: Notre Dame University Press, 1979.

Horn, Chris. *University of South Carolina: A Portrait.* Columbia, S. C.: University of South Carolina Press, 2001.

Horste, Kathryn. *The Michigan Law Quadrangle.* Ann Arbor, Mich: The University of Michigan Press, 1997.

Irish, Sharon. *Cass Gilbert, Architect: Modern Traditionalist.* New York: The Monacelli Press, 1999.

Jeanneret-Gris, Charles Edouard (Le Corbusier). *Quand les cathédrals étaient blanches* (Paris: Plon, 1937), *When the Cathedrals Were White,* trans. Francis E. Hyslop, Jr. (New York: Reynal and Hitchcock, 1947; New York: McGraw-Hill, 1964), 135.

Joncas, Richard, David J. Neumann, and Paul V. Turner. *Stanford University: The Campus Guide.* New York: Princeton Architectural Press, 1999.

Jones, Robert A. *Cass Gilbert: Midwestern Architect in New York.* New York: Arno Press, 1982.

Klauder, Charles Z., and Herbert C. Wise. *College Architecture in America and Its Part in the Development of the Campus.* New York and London: Charles Scribner's Sons, 1929.

Kolowrat, Ernest. *Hotchkiss: A Chronicle of an American School.* New Amsterdam, 1992.

Lanier, Claire Shepherd. *Contextual Eclecticism: Designing Distinctive Campus Architecture for the University of Colorado, 1917–1921.* Denver: University of Colorado at Denver, 2005

Larson, Jens Fredrick, and Archie MacInnes Palmer. *Architectural Planning of the American College.* New York and London: McGraw-Hill, 1933.

Leitch, Alexander. *A Princeton Companion.* Princeton: Princeton University Press, 1978.

Levine, Neil. *The Architecture of Frank Lloyd Wright.* Princeton: Princeton University Press, 1997.

Little, Pat. *Penn State Then and Now.* Lemont, Pennsylvania: Pat Little Photography, 1999.

Lovelace, Richard H. *Mr. Taft's School: The First Century 1890–1990.* Watertown, Conn.: The Taft School, 1989.

Lowell, James Russell. "Harvard Anniversary Address on the Two Hundred and Fiftieth Anniversary of the Foundation of Harvard University," November 8, 1886. *The Complete Writings of James Russell Lowell,* Cambridge, Mass.: Riverside Press, 1904, 170–71.

Lyon, E. Wilson. *The History of Pomona College 1887–1969.* Claremont, Calif.: Pomona College, 1977.

Maddox, Ruth Patterson, ed. *Building SMU 1915–1957: A Warm and Personal Look at the People Who Started Southern Methodist University.* Odenwald Press, 1995.

Maroon, Fred J. *Maroon on Georgetown.* Charlottesville, Va.: Thomasson, Grant & Howell, 1985.

Meacham, Scott. *Dartmouth College: The Campus Guide.* New York: Princeton Architectural Press, 2008.

Mercer, William. *Brown: Images of the University.* Providence, R. I.: Brown University, 2002.

Meisinger, Carol Morris, ed. *University of Pennsylvania: A Photographic Portrait.* Philadelphia: University of Pennsylvania Publications, 1984.

Moody, Barry M. *Give Us an "A": An Acadia Album.* Wolfville, Nova Scotia: Acadia University, 1988.

Morehead, James C. Jr. *A Walking Tour of Rice University.* Houston: Rice University Press, 1984.

Oliver, Richard. *Bertram Grosvenor Goodhue.* Cambridge, Mass.: The MIT Press, 1983.

Osgood, Charles G., Christian Gauss, Hugh Scott Taylor, Robert K. Root, Donald D. Egbert, Walter E. Hope, and Chauncey Belknap. *The Modern Princeton.* Princeton: Princeton University Press, 1947.

Pennoyer, Peter, and Anne Walker. *The Architecture of Delano and Aldrich.* New York and London: W.W. Norton, 2003.

Pettem, Silvia, and Liston E. Leyendecker. *Boulder: Evolution of a City.* Boulder, Colo: University Press of Colorado, 2006.

Pierson, George W. *Yale: A Short History.* New Haven: The Office of the Secretary, Yale University, 1979

Pinnell, Patrick L. *Yale University: The Campus Guide.* New York: Princeton Architectural Press, 1999.

Powell, William S. *The First State University: A Pictorial History of the University of North Carolina* (revised third edition). Chapel Hill and London: The University of North Carolina Press, 1992

Reisler, Mark. *Darden: A Pictorial History of the University of Virginia's Darden Graduate School of Business Administration.* Charlottesville, Va.: Darden Business Publishing, 2005.

Report to Acadia University. New York and Toronto: Taylor, Lieberfeld and Heldman, 1965.

Reynolds, Jon K., and George M. Barringer. *Georgetown University: A Pictorial Review.* Washington, D.C.: Georgetown University Alumni Association, 1976.

Rhinehart, Raymond P. *Princeton University: The Campus Guide.* New York: Princeton Architectural Press, 1999.

Robert A. M. Stern Architects. *College of Notre Dame of Maryland: Master Plan for the Next Century,* 1996.

Rudolph, Frederick. *The American College and University: A History.* New York: Alfred A. Knopf, 1962.

Saarinen, Eero. *Eero Saarinen on His Work,* Aline B. Saarinen, ed., revised edition. New Haven: Yale University Press, 1968.

Sclereth, Thomas J. *The University of Notre Dame: A Portrait of Its History and Campus.* Notre Dame and London: University of Notre Dame, 1976.

Scully, Vincent Jr. *Frank Lloyd Wright.* New York: George Braziller, 1960.

———, Catherine Lynn, Erik Vogt, and Paul Goldberger. *Yale in New Haven: Architecture and Urbanism.* New Haven and London: Yale University Press, 2004.

Shand-Tucci, Douglass. *Harvard University: The Campus Guide.* New York: Princeton Architectural Press, 2001.

Sherwood, P. C., and J. M. Lasala. "Education and architecture: the evolution of the University of Virginia's academic village," in R. G. Wilson, ed., *Thomas Jefferson's Academical Village: The Creation of an Architectural Masterpiece.* Charlottesville, Va.: Bayly Museum of the University of Virginia, distributed by the University of Virginia Press, 1993.

Schuyler, Montgomery. "A Review of the Work of Charles Coolidge Haight" in *Great American Architects Series,* The Architectural Record Co. (New York: Da Capo Press, 1977)

———. "The Architecture of American Colleges I—Harvard." *Architectural Record* 26, no. 4 (October 1909): 243–69.

———. "Architecture of American Colleges II—Yale." *Architectural Record* 26, no. 6 (December 1909): 393–416.

———. "Architecture of American Colleges III—Princeton," *Architectural Record* 27, no. 2 (February 1910): 129–60.

———. "Architecture of American Colleges IV—New York City Colleges," *Architectural Record* 27, no. 6 (June 1910): 442–69.

———. "Architecture of American Colleges V—University of Pennsylvania, Girard, Haverford, Lehigh and Bryn Mawr Colleges," *Architectural Record* 28, no. 3 (September 1910): 182–212.

———."Architecture of American Colleges VI—Dartmouth,

ILLUSTRATION CREDITS

Williams, and Amherst." *Architectural Record* 28, no. 6 (December 1910): 424–42.

———. "Architecture of American Campuses VII—Brown, Bowdoin, Trinity, and Wesleyan." *Architectural Record,* 29, no. 2 (February 1911): 145–66.

———. "Architecture of American Colleges VIII—The Southern Colleges." *Architectural Record* 30, no. 1 (July 1911): 57–84.

Shriver, Phillip R. *Miami University: A Personal History.* Oxford, Ohio: Miami University Press, 1998.

Stern, Robert A. M. *Pride of Place: Building the American Dream.* Boston and New York: Houghton Mifflin Co.; American Heritage, 1986.

———. *Dedication of the Smith Campus Center.* 1999.

———. "The Architecture of St. Paul's School and the Design of the Ohrstrom Library," *Alumni Horae* 72 (Spring 1992) and 73 (Autumn 1992).

Stone, Edward Durell. *The Evolution of an Architect.* New York: Horizon Press, 1962.

Strode, William. *Carolina: A University Portrait.* Columbia, S. C.: University of South Carolina Press, 1986.

Terry, Marshall. *From High on the Hilltop: A Brief History of SMU.* Houston: Southern Methodist University Press, 1993.

Thomas, George E. *University of Pennsylvania: The Campus Guide.* New York: Princeton Architectural Press, 2002.

———. and David B. Brownlee. *Building America's First University: An Historical and Architectural Guide to the University of Pennsylvania.* Philadelphia: University of Pennsylvania Press, 2000.

Truettner, Julia M. *Aspirations for Excellence, Alexander Jackson Davis and the First Plan for the University of Michigan, 1838.* Ann Arbor, Mich.: The University of Michigan Press, 2003.

Turner, Paul Venable. *Campus: An American Planning Tradition.* New York: The Architectural History Foundation, and Cambridge, Mass., and London: The MIT Press, 1984.

Vonada, Damaine. *Notre Dame: The Official Campus Guide.* Notre Dame, Ind.: University of Notre Dame Press, 1998.

Walker, C. Howard."The Inspirational Value of Collegiate Architecture," *The Architectural Forum* 44, no. 6 (June 1926): 345–48.

Willard, Ashton R. "The Development of College Architecture in America." *New England Magazine,* 16, no. 5 (July 1897): 513–34.

Walker, Barbara."Hotchkiss, the Place," *Hotchkiss Magazine,* Spring 2003.

Wills, Garry. *Mr. Jefferson's University.* Washington, D.C.: National Geographic, 2002.

Wilson, Richard Guy, ed.*Thomas Jefferson's Academical Village: The Creation of an Architectural Masterpiece.* Charlottesville, Va.: Bayly Art Museum of the University of Virginia, distributed by University Press of Virginia, 1993.

———. and Sara A. Butler. *University of Virginia: The Campus Guide.* New York: Princeton Architectural Press, 1999.

Woods, Mary N. "Thomas Jefferson and the University of Virginia: Planning the Academical Village." *Journal of the Society of Architectural Historians* 44 (October 1985): 266-83.

Yarnall, James L. *Newport Through Its Architecture: A History of Styles From Postmedieval to Postmodern.* Newport, R. I.: Salve Regina University Press, 2005.

Photographers

Peter Aaron / Esto: 2–3, 10, 23, 26–33, 40–41, 44, 49–56, 61–74, 80–87, 93, 95 (bottom), 96, 101–107, 112, 117–123, 136, 140–146, 152–164, 168–176, 182–183, 186–193, 211, 215–217, 222, 226–234, 239, 241–249, 252, 260–269, 295–297, 300–303, 310, 315–319, 324, 328–337, 346, 350–363, 370–377, 392, 396–401, 414, 420–429, 432, 436–437, 440–444, 448–454, 458–464, 468–472, 474–476, 480–489, 492, 497–502, 507–514, 518–519, 522–526, 530–531, 534–537, 546, 550–558, 562–571

Richard Bryant: 88, 95 (top)
Francis Dzikowski / Esto: 16, 34–39, 338–345, 364, 368–369, 378–387, 406–413
Tina Hay: 520
Chris Kendall: 202, 208–209, 212–214
Jack Looney: 24
James A. Marshall: 14–15
Michael Marsland: 298
Jock Pottle: 124, 130, 134–135
Pictrometry International Corporation: 473
Albert Večerka / Esto: 270–271, 273, 276–281

Renderers

Michael McCann: 129, 132–133, 282–285, 320
Thomas Schaller: 108
Jeff Stikeman: 194, 198, 286, 304–309, 538, 543–545

Reference Images

University of Virginia Dan Grogan: 18 (right); Timothy Hursley: 20 (below); Courtesy University of Virginia Library: 18 (above, below); Courtesy Princeton Architectural Press: 19 (above) **The College of William and Mary** Courtesy College of William and Mary Archives: 46 (above) **University of South Carolina** Courtesy Historic Columbia Foundation: 58 (above); **Stanford University** Jill Clardy: 76 (above); Courtesy Princeton Architectural Press: 76 (right, bottom right) **University of California, Irvine** Steve Owen: 90 (above); Courtesy University of California, Irvine: 90 (right) **Columbia University** Peter Mauss / Esto: 99 (above); Courtesy Cameron and Company: 98 (above); Courtesy New-York Historical Society: 98 (below) **Bronx Community College** Thomas Schaller: 111 (left above); McKim, Mead and White monograph: 110 (above); Courtesy New York University Archives: 110 (right) **Johns Hopkins University** Courtesy Johns Hopkins University: 114 (left); Courtesy Ayers Saint Gross: 115 (left) **Southern Methodist University** Courtesy Southern Methodist University: 126 (above), 127 (left) **University of Nebraska, Lincoln** Ezra Stoller / Esto: 138 (right) **Rice University** Courtesy Rice University: 148 (below) **Indiana University/Purdue University** Courtesy Indiana University/Purdue University: 166 (right) **Pomona College** Courtesy Pomona College: 178–179, 180 (top) **University of Notre Dame** Jeff Stikeman: 196 (below) **Franklin and Marshall College** Courtesy Franklin and Marshall College: 200 (above) **The Hotchkiss School** Courtesy Hotchkiss School: 204, 206 (right, below) **University of Colorado at Boulder** Courtesy University of Colorado at Boulder: 220 (below) **Florida Southern College** Robin Hill: 236; Courtesy Florida Southern College: 237 (above right); Courtesy Frank Lloyd Wright Foundation: 237 (above left, left) **Harvard University** Jonathan Wallen: 255 (left); Courtesy Princeton Architectural Press: 254 (above, below right), 255 (below), 257 (below), 258; Courtesy Havard University Press: 254 (below left), 256 (above), 257 (above)**Yale University** Steve Dunwell: 291 (above right);

Courtesy Yale University: 288, 289 (above), 290 (above, right), 291 (above right), 292–293 **University of Pennsylvania** Getty Images: 313 (above); Courtesy Detroit Publishing Company: 312 (above) **Brown University** Michael McCann: 322 (below), 323; Courtesy Brown University: 322 (top left, top right, left)**University of Michigan** Nick Sortzi: 326 (above) **Brooklyn Law School** Peter Aaron / Esto: 348 (above); Courtesy PropertyShark: 348 (right) **Salve Regina University** Courtesy Cornell University Library: 366 (bottom left) **University of California Los Angeles** Ernest Burden III: 390 (below); Courtesy UCLA Health System: 388, 391 (left, below); **Dartmouth College** Michael McCann: 394 (below); Courtesy Dartmouth College: 394 (above) **Miami University** Tim Jones: 404 (above right) **St. Paul's School** Courtesy The MIT Press: 418 (right bottom); Courtesy St. Paul's School: 419 (top, above)**Georgetown University** Kiah Patzkowsky: 434 (above); Courtesy Georgetown University Archives: 434 (above) **Trinity University** Peter Aaron / Esto: 446 (below middle); James Wilson: 446 (below right); Courtesy University of Texas Press: 446 (above) **College of Notre Dame of Maryland** Courtesy College of Notre Dame of Maryland: 456 (above, below left, below right, below) **Ithaca College** Courtesy Sasaki: 478 (above) **Princeton University** Dan Beards: 494 (above) **University of North Carolina Chapel Hill** Thomas Schaller: 505 (above); Courtesy University of North Carolina Press: 504 (below), 505 (left) **Pennsylvania State University** Courtesy Pennsylvania State University: 516 (right, below left) **Acadia University** Peter Aaron / Esto: 528 (bottom); **Marist College** Aerial Photos of New Jersey: 540 (above); Jeff Stikeman: 541 **California State University Northridge** Courtesy University Archives, California State University: 548 (above); **University of Nevada Las Vegas** Geri Kodey: 560 (above); Courtesy University of Nevada Las Vegas: 560 (right)